James Vodnik was born in Milwaukee in 1949 to a Catholic mother and an Agnostic father, this oldest of five grew up in a poor, working-class neighborhood. A shy child, intensely curious, asking questions, challenging elders and the status quo, early on wondering, 'Who am I?' and 'Why am I here?' He delivered newspapers as a boy and helped the family financially.

He graduated with honors from UWM with a Bachelor of Arts degree in Psychology and Philosophy. Concurrently, he was a Conscientious Objector to the Vietnam War. As a Zen practitioner, the desire for truth and meaning prompted a lifelong study of the human condition.

To my dear wife, Theda, who spent countless hours reading and editing this book when I am sure she could have found better things to do with her time! I owe you one, honey. And a sincere thanks to my younger brother, Gregory, the poet, for his thoughtful, wise advice in helping me in choosing a title for this effort.

Again, much gratitude to my erudite friend, Kirk, for the benefit of his masterful word-smithing suggestions! And finally, thanks to my friend, Robin, artist par excellence, for her insightful ideas.

James Vodnik

HUMANITY IN TROUBLE AND OUR FAILURE TO ACT

Critical Warnings, Insights, Jabs and Solutions

AUSTIN MACAULEY PUBLISHERS™
LONDON • CAMBRIDGE • NEW YORK • SHARJAH

Ordering Information
Quantity sales: Special discounts are available on quantity purchases by corporations, associations, and others. For details, contact the publisher at the address below.

Publisher's Cataloging-in-Publication data
Vodnik, James
Humanity in Trouble and Our Failure to Act

ISBN 9798889105404 (Paperback)
ISBN 9798889105978 (ePub e-book)

Library of Congress Control Number: 2023920611

www.austinmacauley.com/us

First Published 2024
Austin Macauley Publishers LLC
40 Wall Street, 33rd Floor, Suite 3302
New York, NY 10005
USA

mail-usa@austinmacauley.com
+1 (646) 5125767

Table of Contents

Introduction   9

Chapter 1: Starting Out Light. Pet Peeves   13

Chapter 2: United We Stand but Divided
       Makes More Sense   21

Chapter 3: Who Speaks for Earth?   28

Chapter 4: Fake Hollywood, Believe Half of
       What You See…   36

Chapter 5: Feeling Good: The Prime Directive   49

Chapter 6: You Really Are What You Eat!   53

Chapter 7: It's All About Me   60

Chapter 8: The Secret of True Health Revealed   68

Chapter 9: Problems with the News   76

Chapter 10: Understanding the Self   83

Chapter 11: The Failure of Democracy   93

Chapter 12: The Myth of Intelligence   103

Chapter 13: The Truth About Capitalism   107

Chapter 14: The Failure to Teach Life Skills   111

Chapter 15: The Big Scary
            Bogeyman SOCIALISM!   119

Chapter 16: The 1% Are Responsible for
            Global Warming   124

Chapter 17: US Constitution Woefully Obsolete!   131

Chapter 18: Unvironmentalism   143

Chapter 19: You Really Can't Fix Stupid   147

Chapter 20: Do Robots Have Feelings?   151

Chapter 21: The Death of Grammar   158

Chapter 22: More Crap That Doesn't
            Make Any Sense   164

Chapter 23: Attention White Supremacists:
            'We're All Black!'   174

Chapter 24: So Long It's Been Good to Know Ya... 180

Chapter 25: I Strongly Recommend...   192

Introduction

Let me start by saying I really wanted to title this book WTF (what the F&#@*%^) is wrong with humanity but I chickened out, worried that the vulgar, colloquial language would alienate potential readers and quite possibly result in a useful work being censored and deemed unpublishable, despite our First Amendment rights.

However, my original inspiration for starting this writing project was my frequent and on-going incredulity, outrage, and disappointment with my fellow man that more often than not left me with the intellectual and emotional reaction of "WTF". I know there are many more of us who feel the same way and forgive me if I am being repetitive, overly obvious, and beating the dog to death, but I was compelled to get things off my chest in a reasonably constructive manner.

With that in mind, you will continue to see the afore-stated acronym used periodically in this book and hope you are not offended.

As if there isn't already enough BS going around and I mean everywhere, why would I add to it? What qualifies me to comment on the state of humanity and the planet? Well, for one thing, I notice things, both stupid and untrue, in the mainstream media, both video and radio, social media, print, entertainment, government, politics, medicine, religion, and education. And I am pretty fed up and feel compelled to vent, to expose, to correct and call out the unqualified, mean-spirited, greedy, and most importantly evil manipulators in the world.

And to top it all off, a never-ending stream of incompetence and ignorance is flooding our brainwaves and offered up for sale and unreserved consumption to the human psyche. Sometimes I wish there was a God to keep things in check, to keep us from going too far afield from our given purpose for existing (WTF?) and straying too far from nature. I am lamenting the human condition from the perspective of a citizen of the USA but a similar rant could be proffered by a resident of virtually any nation.

However, let me say this at the onset, all this baloney about the United States of America being the greatest nation on Earth, what a crock, what arrogance! That may once have been the case but we forfeited that title years ago, I am guessing sometime during the Vietnam War. If indeed we ever held it, or any nation realistically can, or who gives a damn and what difference does it make, anyway?

Again, what is the point of writing a book that attempts to explain the major problems created by and facing humanity? Well, for one thing, and actually the main thing, I just don't see much being done to fix this sick planet or wake up humanity on a scale broad enough to keep the train on the tracks.

Does it even matter? You wouldn't think so judging from the state of the Earth's environment and the geo-political climate. We have these incredible brains, able to unravel the mysteries of the universe and perceive our status as galactic citizens but we can't keep mountains of trash out of our oceans. We can't stop killing one another, we can't stop breeding in excess, we can't stop brutalizing nature, and on and on. We need to wake the hell up before it is too late and man, it just might be too late.

Still, we gotta try. Clearly, the greatest problem facing us is global warming, that's right, global warming, and I will not only use the politically correct term "climate change" as that just makes it easier for deniers and believers alike to do nothing and instead focus on buying their gas-guzzling, greenhouse gas-spewing SUVs and RVs.

In fact, why don't we be honest and call it what it really is, "global overheating"! Pretty scary, huh? But that is what it is and seemingly expressing the harsh truth may be the only way to prompt the masses to action.

How can "we" be so stupid? And I am talking about the big WE, all humanity. Enough of us have transcended the stone age and the struggle to survive, have devised technologies for safe shelter and uninterrupted food production so as to ensure the survival of our species, presumably freeing up enough brain power to address and solve global, environmental, political, racial and religious problems.

Whether or not one is a believer, atheist or agnostic, we have an absolute responsibility to alleviate suffering, not only for our fellow humans but for all life, both plant and animal. Nature has not endowed us with spectacular brains and bodies only to become food bags and killing machines.

The sentience we are endowed with, or shall I say randomly enabled with, since so many of us exhibit virtually no evidence of awareness, represents the material universe waking up, seeing itself, perhaps for the first time and we are morally bound to honor and advance that phenomenal new dimension called consciousness!

It goes without saying right? Or one could argue that Nature, the Cosmos, Creation, and God don't give a damn. We are free (apparently) to screw things up, to over-eat, over-populate, over-produce, over-consume, over-kill and so what?

Well, I, for one, am outraged about the condition of the planet, all of life and legacy of humanity but before I offer solutions I have a need to rant and expose some of our folly and ignorance in the hope of setting the record straight while amusing myself and hopefully you my reader in the process. Virtually every thought, word and deed that will be excoriated in this book will inevitably support the notion that you "can't fix stupid".

Lastly, while I am virtually certain that it will become glaringly obvious early on, if not already, this book does not purport to be an academic work but rather represents an opinionated, reasonably educated, carefully considered editorial on society and the human condition. I humbly offer a variety of insights, suggestions for correcting our mistakes, a glimmer of hope and ultimately a path to bequeathing a habitable planet to our grandchildren.

Chapter 1
Starting Out Light. Pet Peeves

There are so many stupid statements, dumb actions and downright unbelievable, moronic moves being made all the time by people that get attention first hand and in the various media and this has been the case as long as I can remember. *Some are not much of a big deal but others have consequences and they have been annoying me so I just have to say something out loud in the spirit of WTF, so bear with me as I set the record straight on just a few.*

"I said to myself".

We hear this all the time, especially when TV reporters are interviewing people for a story. When you examine this statement, it is pretty dumb and perpetuates the myth that there is a little man or woman inside your head that "you" are actually talking to. The same as "thinking to myself". How about you are simply "thinking"?

Because that is all you are doing. Or better yet, you are just witnessing thoughts arise because, in fact, that is what is primarily happening. We are responsible for at best a small percentage of thoughts occurring in our brains and our primary duty, and our privilege, is to filter or edit. Not take all the nonsense our brains crank out too seriously. Nor to identify with or act out the gobbledy gook that arises, I call that mentally ill. I would ask all individuals who "say to myself" or "think to myself" who, what and where is this SELF that you are speaking to?

"I forgive you".

You just murdered my husband, raped my daughter, or rammed my car in an act of road rage. I find it in my heart to forgive you. Have you apologized? NO! In my opinion, it is pointless to forgive somebody for committing an evil, vile, criminal act when they haven't offered an unsolicited apology!

That is not true forgiveness, but rather an act of assuaging your own pain and loss. Try grief therapy or mourning, that is what a person really needs. Forgiving an unapologetic evildoer does nothing to enlighten that person, but rather minimizes the seriousness of their act and virtually blesses the commission of future crimes. Best to let them squirm and see the suffering they have wrought. With luck, they will have an epiphany.

However, if you must, then go ahead and "love thine enemy" but don't forgive them without a heartfelt, unsolicited apology.

'How cops get extra vacations?'

Listen up people, I mean you and me and all citizens and taxpayers. All a cop has to do these days to get an unplanned, paid vacation is shoot a black man! That's right, just shoot a black man; they don't have to catch them in the act of committing a crime, maybe just have a reason to detain or pull them over, for one reason or another.

Nine times out of ten when a cop shoots a black man, he (rarely she) gets paid administrative leave! This is unbelievable. It is an outrage and a slap in the face of the family of the shooting victim and to anyone with a conscience. Yet, I don't hear an outcry from any quarter, politicians or victims alike; perhaps the media simply doesn't report it.

WE are, in essence, rewarding cops who shoot blacks and I believe this should also be taken up by the Black Lives Matter movement. It is unconscionable. Now I suppose in a very few instances, and I mean very, very few, the shootings may be legitimate, say in the case of an armed robber.

However, as we have come to see via the occasional release of body cam footage and perhaps more often the release of bystander cell phone videos, the black men are unarmed, hands up, in the act of surrender. In a few cases, they may be fleeing and who can blame them, there is a strong possibility that they will get the crap kicked out of them or shot. Here's a novel thought: *why not put the shooter cop on desk duty instead of rewarding them with administrative leave, or suspend them without pay?*

'Shoot to Kill.'

While we are on the subject of cops shooting "suspects," it is appropriate to bring up another serious problem with policing and that is the use of deadly force. Cops are trained in the use of firearms so I assume they know how to aim a handgun.

Is there anybody who can tell me why they shoot suspects, especially those fleeing, in the back or the chest, and on top of that multiple times? Why can't they just shoot them in the leg or arm? Or better yet, not shoot at all and instead use their taser, and not multiple times sending the victim into cardiac arrest. It would seem there are a lot of really frightened cops out there or in the least very poorly trained.

"Cop Killers, Two Wrongs Don't Make a Right".

Just as tragic and evil as a cop shooting a fleeing black teen or a "driving while black person," is the case of the black (or white), random, cop killer. What the heck is wrong with these people? It doesn't even the score or stop the bad, racist cops from acting out violently.

In fact, it just angers cops all the more and makes them nervous and more likely to overreact when confronting a black citizen. And how does the cop killer know he is shooting a racist cop? It could be, and most likely, is the case that they are killing a good cop and hurting the BLM movement as well.

"Invest in Disease".

What a crazy thought but that is what the health insurance system does in the USA, it is run as a for-profit enterprise with the complete endorsement of the big pharmaceuticals and healthcare institutions. Is it any wonder health insurance premiums, drugs and medical costs are through the roof?

Some of the highest on the planet! Take the raw cost of providing coverage and jack it 30–50% to pay stockholder dividends and huge executive salaries. Oh, and don't forget what the insurers pay lobbyists in DC. We are getting screwed. Premiums and deductibles keep going up. I wonder what the pandemic is going to do to the consumer's pocketbook? Just wait. Maybe single payer (evil socialism) won't look so bad! **"Stupid Hikers"**

Do you ever wonder what some people are thinking when they set off on a back country hike by themselves? Perhaps calling it "thinking" is too generous a characterization. Do they check the weather forecast? No. Do they notify friends, relatives or park rangers of their route? No. Do they take a cell phone? Maybe, but there is less than a 50% chance they will have service. Do they have a plan for dealing with an injury such as a broken ankle? Or how they will react when confronted by a bear or mountain lion?

There are a lot of other things that could be mentioned but you get the point. Bottom line is it annoys me to no end that WE, the taxpayers, end up paying to mount massive search and rescue initiatives through the Park Service or local fire and rescue departments. And when they are rescued, I never hear an apology for upsetting anyone who cares or adequate appreciation for the rescuers. It's all about me.

"Gawker's Block/Poor Sonsabitches"!

Ever find yourself driving along the interstate or freeway and see vehicles heading in the opposite direction at a dead stop, all lanes piled up with cars and trucks, hundreds of souls feeling hopelessly trapped, late for work, late for dinner, worried about running out of gas, having to pee real bad and perhaps most of all wondering what the hell is going on?

You whizzed by too quickly, I hope, to see what is going on but thanked your lucky stars it was them and not you. But you feel their pain and utter frustration since you have been there before! Poor sonsabitches you think to yourself and say a little prayer that the same fate doesn't befall you and all your compatriots driving in the other direction.

Here's the rub, when they finally get to the source of the problem, it's just some schmuck changing a flat on the shoulder and everybody just had to slow down and look for some blood. And if you're having a really bad day, both directions will be backed up because all the fools on your side are just slowing down to see what is happening on the other side! Idiots! I just can't wait for autonomous cars and smart roads. And maybe even smart cops who don't shut down the whole freaking highway for something that happened in one lane.

"Never a Supervisor Be"!

Of course we all want and need to make more money and one way to do that is moving up in the company by becoming a *supervisor*. You're on your way, a 30% bump in pay, no punching the clock or somebody looking over your shoulder and finally on the fast track to a successful career and some real money.

Sounds pretty good, right? Well, listen up friend, it is not all it is cracked up to be and in fact it can be living hell and all the money in the world isn't worth the pain and suffering. Unless you get really lucky and get a crew composed entirely of intelligent, honest, sincere people, you are pretty much fucked. In my 45+ year working life (yes I am retired, smartest thing I ever did), those periods during which I was a supervisor or manager and had "directs" were without a doubt some of the worst periods of my life without exception.

Now, it is entirely possible I contributed to some of the problems I encountered but am not responsible for the darker, devious, dishonest side of human nature and you get to see it all and deal with it as a supervisor. Some examples include:

- Theft of company property, a real popular one.
- Chronic tardiness, fake calling in sick.
- Poor performance.
- Retribution for giving an honest but poor performance review.
- Plotting mutiny and sabotage by subordinates.
- Incompetent job applicants who lie about their experience.
- Lack of accountability, a "give a shit" attitude.
- Threatened by a disgruntled worker with a gun.
- Lack of support from your bosses, perhaps the worst.

I could probably write a chapter filled with just my supervisor horror stories, mishaps and misadventures but I think you get the point.

Please take this warning seriously if you are contemplating taking that promotion. You better have a steel will, limitless courage and possibly a license to carry. You never know when somebody will go Postal. Seriously.

"Infants left in cars".

How in God's name can a person forget they left their kid in the car? Simple answer, they can't or don't and in many cases they are just trying to get rid of a responsibility they never imagined a child could be. Oh, I guess there may be a few cases where they are not trying to murder the kid; they are impossibly stupid, have narcissistic personality disorder, ADHD or are mentally ill.

However, those that leave children in cars need to be punished with hard time and prevented from having any more kids. And what about any remaining children in that household? I think child protective services should intervene and remove them to a safe foster or adoptive home.

"Pets in cars".

While not a dog lover, I can't help but be disturbed by this cruel, stupid act of neglect. So often you hear of people leaving their pets in cars on a hot summer day and even with the windows cracked, this can be fatal. And if and when they are caught doing this, there should be a large fine and even some jail time along with losing their "Pet Permit".

Of course, this is not the only abuse committed by pet owners, let's not forget dropping puppies in dumpsters, abandoning kittens alongside a country highway, starvation and the neglect of leaving Fido chained up outside 24/7. Very sad!

Chapter 2
United We Stand but Divided
Makes More Sense

The fact is, we are the United States of America in name only anymore. Granted, I am not a storehouse of American history but as I see it you would have to go back to revolutionary times to find a period when the States were united in practice and principle.

As the 13 Colonies grew into a nation and more states were recognized, a major schism grew around the practice of slavery and in a little over 60 years the pro-slavery states, "the South" violently attempted to secede from the union resulting in a bloody civil war in which over 500,000 died.

As we all know, the South lost and Lincoln and the North put an official end to slavery but the South refused to accept this and the mindset of white supremacy persists to this day in a form of incipient racism, black voter suppression through gerrymandered congressional districts and most recently minority voter suppression in Republican controlled state houses.

Sadly, the civil war continues to be fought even to this day only the front has changed from the bloody battlefield to the US Congress, the Red State (mostly Southern) Houses and overt racism and segregation in Red State institutions.

Let's be real, what the heck is going on in "our" country? The 2020 national election and January 6 Capital insurrection sadly point to the fact that we are not united, not one nation and no amount of debate or calls for unity will ever change that. The ideological gulf between Americans exemplified by the two majority political parties has become a chasm that will never be bridged.

The civil war was won but it never quite ended and is still being fought on local, state, and national fronts with increasing rancor. What has been going on for the past 50+ years politically in the country, for my entire adult voting life, has been a see-saw battle for control that always left one half of the population somewhat content and the other half frustrated and angry for at least four years.

The insurrection of January 6 came close to triggering or should I say, "reigniting" civil war. The hate filled, violent sentiments expressed on that day are simply not going away, ever. So what should we do? Group therapy? Peace talks?

We need to wake up to the fact that there are too many beliefs that divide us and it is time to craft a political solution that allows the two major factions in this country to form their own independent, political subdivisions. It is time for red and blue states, counties and cities to go their separate ways. It is clear that after almost 250 years, sharing the same geography and national border does not make a nation.

Quite a disturbing notion, right? We are the United States of America, bastion of liberty, greatest democracy in history, model to the world. But after almost 250 years, a flaw in the concept of democracy has become glaringly obvious and, over time, increasingly hard to ignore.

In fact, we are at a point where it is dangerous to ignore the extreme, political, ideological disharmony so deeply embedded in our land. Take the Obama administration's years years in the Whitehouse, where at first the primary goal of the Republican Party was to render him a one-term president and failing that, thwart his and the democrat's every move without a hint of cooperation or compromise as the Founders intended.

The extreme polarization has rendered the majority in the Congress unable to govern and work to solve the urgent problems facing the nation. Take also the case of the Republican controlled Senate's refusal to give Obama's Supreme Court nominee a fair hearing and a vote, as the Constitution stipulates they must. Unfair, unprecedented and un-American!

What is the point of going on the way we are? We value individual liberty and the pursuit of happiness but with the deep moral, economic, religious, racial and political animosity across our land, advancing the agenda of one party always seems to diminish or at least threaten the objectives of the other, resulting in perpetual discord.

Feelings of resentment and hopelessness and even hatred have grown so strong and run so deep politically and culturally that dialogue has broken down and working out differences has become virtually impossible. Compromise is no longer acceptable to either party and in most instances has become impossible between them alas, and we have the resultant permanent gridlock.

Therefore, it is time to admit the "great experiment" the United States of America, has failed and the gridlock and animosity that prevails across the land has become so toxic that if we don't make some radical changes soon, things will get increasingly divisive and broad social unrest and violence will spread across the land.

The term "culture wars" has become part of the vernacular and for very good reason. As the population of our nation has grown, so has racial, religious, political, cultural, technological and gender diversity.

We are no longer able to cluster in communities that share belief systems, as was marginally possible in the early years of the union. As a result of increasing urbanization, divergent cultural groups are coming in close contact with and competition for resources and the dominant culture, WASP, is unwilling to share the wealth and subsequently we have become a nation of haves and have nots.

Add to this mix the conglomeration and monopolization of wealth in the hands of the 1% and the masses find themselves in a perpetual state of struggle and financial hardship. In order to be heard and compete, the many subcultures organize as neighborhoods, social media movements and voting blocks and thus culture wars have become the status quo. We see this on a national and global scale as exemplified by the mass exodus of refugees to the West resulting from "Arab Spring".

We have had brutal oppression of African Americans within our own border for hundreds of years, and that persists to this day at the hands of systemic racist police departments and culturally biased legislative, educational and economic institutions. With the ever increasing racial and religious diversification resulting from our heretofore open immigration policies, we have seen this oftentimes violent, racist oppression spread to Asian, Hispanic and Muslim minorities.

We are on the verge of becoming a failed state and need to act before it is too late! We need to form something similar to the EU, call it the North American Union (NAU). And we can call the newly reorganized subdivisions the Conservative States of America (CSA) and the Liberal States of America (LSA). Maybe call the LSA, the SSA, (Socialist States of America), HA.

SSA is also the Social Security Administration, perfect parallel. Along with Medicare and Medicaid, how many conservatives are ready to give up those social programs? Hypocrites!

When you think of it, the existing state borders are obsolete given the rise of massive urban political entities such as LA, NYC, Houston and Chicago. These should be recognized as city-states. We can subsequently gerrymander new state borders to group like population centers into LSAs and CSAs. The new states, city states and nations don't have to be geographically contiguous since many of the original institutions and laws will continue to be shared including trade, environment, infrastructure and defense.

Of course, reinventing the nation will be complicated but the opposing sides will have a vested interest in making it work since the process will put the avarice to rest, remove the threat of a second civil war once and for all.

Of course creating a new union with two separate major national subdivisions, separate constitutions and a treaty call it WATO (West Atlantic Treaty Organization) will be an enormous task and the US Constitution will have to be updated completely and revised, if not discarded and totally rewritten. Blasphemy you say? No, just common sense.

Along with the Bill of Rights, these documents are obsolete and major revisions are needed to reflect the many social, scientific and legal advancements that have been made in 250 years. This would also be the time to recognize all American territories, such as Puerto Rico, Guam and US Virgin Islands as fully vested members in the union of their choice.

Furthermore, each new union of states/city states would have its own executive, Congress or parliament, along with a separate judiciary. A good time too to create fair tax codes, I suggest eliminating the income tax and adopting a national sales tax for personal and business, simple and fair to all, progressive, no loopholes and eliminates the need for the bloated IRS! And let's not forget term limits for all public office and the elimination of private campaign contributions and removal of the undue, corrupt influence of lobbyists!

I realize what I am proposing here may seem unrealistic and may be considered by some as anti-American but let's face it, the road we are traveling down politically and socially is one of total gridlock, impotent government and growing, violent social unrest. We need to read the writing on the wall and soon.

What happened during the Trump Presidency was a glaring, reckless drift toward the Fascism of Hitler and this was demonstrated beyond doubt by the Trump's "Big Lie" inspired insurrection on January 6, 2021!

The political, social, racial, sexual and religious acrimony in our nation continues to spread as diversity grows. There is no meeting of the minds, no blending of social and political institutions with the vast differences between the various subgroups represented in our borders and anyone who cannot see that is avoiding reality. With a little luck and ingenuity, perhaps we can save the dream that once was the United States of America and really create a more perfect pair of unions!

Chapter 3
Who Speaks for Earth?

Damn, where to start? I am so overwhelmed with anger and disappointment at the condition of our precious Earth and what WE have done to it in 300 years. We have brought the survival of our species to the brink of extinction as a result of the massive overuse of fossil fuels and to what end? The creation of a selfish, wasteful, global consumer society? The pursuit of wealth and luxury? Cellphones and Facebook for seven billion? What idiocy!

In this great experiment, nature has produced life on a cold rock orbiting an average star in a typical galaxy against massive odds. And this life has, over several billion years evolved in so many wonderful ways and the pièce de résistance is an upright, big-brained, bipedal creature that has evolved to manifest sentience, is self-aware or shall I say capable of being self-aware.

The universe has evolved the Fifth Dimension, "consciousness" and is now aware of itself, has the intelligence to look deeply into its operations and unravel the mysteries of creation and no longer is an inanimate, material, quantum soup.

What an amazing accomplishment, what a huge opportunity, the universe is our oyster, we are at the doorstep of the galaxy and the potential to evolve into "gods" and what are we doing with this gift from nature? We are squandering it! And we better get our shit together real soon or else we will bring about our own extinction along with thousands of other unfortunate species who just happened to be in the wrong place at the right time.

Perhaps I should have titled this chapter "who speaks for mankind" since the problems for Earth seem to be solely the result of human activity. And to clarify, I don't mean the rocky planet, its fate is at the mercy of the Sun or some massive, wayward space rock that falls into its gravity.

Of course, I am referring to life on Earth. Who speaks for all those beautiful, amazing plants and creatures? The unmitigated arrogance and greed we exhibit in how we conduct our affairs, reproduce out of control and waste resources. By the way, whatever happened to ZPG? Zero Population Growth.

From Paul Erlich's great book, *The Population Bomb*. We've had over 50 years to consider his warning of famine and political chaos and based on his arguments we must conclude that the Earth can only "comfortably" sustain 5–7 billion humans, and we have exceeded that limit already. Judging from the political chaos, pandemics, famines and environmental crisis currently the norm, he was absolutely right. Instead of reproducing responsibly, we continued breeding like rabbits, out of control.

That, along with a complete disregard for the sustainable use of natural resources, especially harmful fossil fuels, has left us with a big, fucking planet heating, sea level rising, extreme weather event, record forest fire season, polluted mess!

Recently, there has been much ado about the release of videos by the US government of videos showing purported UFO's, now more scientifically termed unidentified aerial phenomenon (UAP).

The release of this information, I won't call it evidence, at this time in the history of humanity, forces one to conclude there is absolutely no chance of aliens having visited Earth since any level 3 civilization would have either stepped in to help us fix this massive mess we have created or they would have removed homo sapiens (wise man) for violation of the terms of our lease. We are destroying the property and injuring/killing our neighbors.

My god, can you imagine the film *The Day the Earth Stood Still* and the alien stepping out and asking to see the leader of the planet and our answer is "we don't have a leader". How embarrassing that would be, how impossibly stupid we would seem when asked 'who is responsible for the upkeep and protection of this planet?'

You may ask me how naïve can you be to assert there can and should be a leader for the Earth? Well, given the human "condition" that may be true but having an effective global leader or leadership council (UN?) is simply common sense and the only viable way to get our house in order, given the widely divergent religious, political, cultural and economic conditions across the planet.

But apparently, we have no common sense or general sense as a species or, in fact, as individuals and I will address the death of common sense in a later chapter.

So it seems the answer to the question posed by this chapter is, **'no one speaks for Earth!'** That being the case, given the dire state of affairs with the planet rapidly overheating, the resultant ocean acidification, rising sea levels, extreme weather events, food chain disruption and on and on, we have very little time left, perhaps 30 years, to significantly reduce greenhouse gas emissions, halt or even reverse global warming and prevent the next extinction event, ours!

That is a huge problem and unless WE anoint, appoint, elect or some other way put some benevolent, wise, charismatic individual or council in charge of humanity's activities, we are screwed. Sadly, the chances of creating an enlightened, global government or at minimum a socially, environmentally focused world council are dim.

We have had one, i.e., the United Nations, for over 70 years and unfortunately it has had at best a minimal impact. Certainly not enough authority to avert perpetual warfare, genocide, starvation, overpopulation and environmental degradation. What seems to be the problem? I'll tell you.

The vast majority of the human race is governed by the primal "instinct" to survive, the effect of that drive rendering most of us motivated by greed, inability to control anger and guided by delusional thinking.

While the survival instincts were essential for our species to evolve over several million years, survive as a potential prey species for large predators and compete for and secure adequate food supplies, these very same traits cloud our ability to think and reason, which evolved much later. It is a shame to see that the amazing brains nature has endowed us with are, for the most part dominated by the baser instincts.

In fact, the most prevalent type of economic system, capitalism, is first and foremost based on competition and greed. We can see what this egocentric focus has done to humanity and the environment over the past couple of thousand years. Endless wars and genocide. Mindless reproduction resulting in vastly over populating the planet and to the point of exhausting resources, 3/4 of the human race living in extreme poverty and squalor. And the situation only continues to get worse with the global population approaching eight billion.

To further complicate matters, our "intelligence" has enabled us to develop technology with means of production of food, goods, services and warfare that are inorganic, resource intensive (wasteful) highly polluting and deadly. And there are for all intents and purposes no controls over the quantities and consequences of the vast industries that we have developed and in fact, I would offer that technology **is out of control**.

Tech and industry have become self-perpetuating and this out of control economic engine is directly responsible for global environmental degradation, resource depletion and excess production of trillions of tons of planet warming greenhouse gases. All for the creation of an overwhelming supply of consumer junk, all for the creation of untold wealth for the few.

With profit (greed) as its guiding principle, and growth as a necessary adjunct of sales and profit, WE have unwittingly evolved a system that has become a runaway train which is hurtling humanity toward extinction.

Nature has given us the tools, intelligence and sentience that have enabled us to ensure survival of our species but our baser instincts, greed, anger and delusion have impeded and ultimately clouded our judgement and ability as a species to control tech. The mad, powerful, insatiable tech genie is out of the bottle.

It doesn't take a genius, an economist, an evolutionary biologist or philosopher of science to see that we have created a real serious shit storm on our home planet. Kudos to Elon Musk and Jeff Bezos and NASA for striving to colonize Mars but given our dire situation on Earth and the fact that we haven't attained level one civilization status, their aspirations are quite premature.

In fact, the massive greenhouse gas emissions created by this industry are just another unnecessary addition to our planet overheating! The logical and wise path would be to dedicate a majority of our tech and industry to solving the dual problems of over-population and severe, extinction level global warming.

In fact, whether we like it or not, whether we know it or not, we have an obligation to abide by Nature's Laws! It boggles my mind that WE don't see this. Oh, of course, many do, perhaps millions, but that is not nearly enough. Simply providing food, shelter and life's appurtenances for 7.5 billion, especially given our unsustainable means of production, continues to worsen the problem exponentially.

So, nature will deal with us and soon if we continue to ignore her laws and sadly, we will take down a lot of other precious, beautiful living creatures (think Manatees) and plants with us.

The title of this chapter is "Who Speaks for Earth" but that raises another conundrum, which is 'who speaks for humanity?' What was intended by the first statement is who or what advocates for and protects the biosphere and all the elements, oceans, plants and animals on it.

By the later what I am getting at is whom, either what individual(s) agency or government makes decisions and is accountable for the collective activities of our species? Quite clearly the answer is no one and no thing! What if, as so many think, aliens checking out our planet finally get up the nerve, get over their shyness and actually ask 'take me to your leader,' what would we do? Who would we send them to? Who would take responsibility for the mess we have made and offer some kind of rationale?

Well, clearly we have no individual or council or cabal of any sort that could step in. Pathetic right? And embarrassing. Quite frankly I am embarrassed to call myself a member of the human race and, as a galactic citizen, am embarrassed for us all!

Given the 7.5 billion points of view and divergent desires and perhaps the few (thousand?) who actually hold the power and sway over the destiny of mankind and the fate of the planet and their many competing interests, disagreements on such things as science and human rights, it is naïve to think that any group could ever make intelligent, humane and sustainable decisions for the planet.

So, we find ourselves in a quandary. The only way to save the planet, specifically much of life as we know it including ourselves, is to come to a broad consensus on what to do asap to halt global warming along with how to implement those activities world-wide. It is possible at least theoretically but the catch is that there is no effective global leadership nor is there consensus among influencers and governments as to the existence, cause or cure for runaway climate change.

This state of affairs has been allowed to persist and in fact worsen, in spite of a continual and growing preponderance of scientific evidence identifying human sourced greenhouse gas emissions since the dawn of the industrial revolution as the primary reason for the more recent, rapid, increasing global temperature, rising sea levels and extreme weather events.

However, despite our history of conflict and the seeming irreversible state of planetary overheating, I do believe the situation is not hopeless and have several recommendations for what can and should be done immediately, which I will take up in a subsequent chapter.

Chapter 4
Fake Hollywood, Believe Half of What You See...

The old adage "Believe half of what you see and none of what you hear" that is attributed to Benjamin Franklin and later Edgar Allan Poe and most recently (1960) Mr. Karman my 5th grade math teacher, is very wise advice indeed, especially useful and I would even say, necessary when dealing with Hollywood and the media in general.

I know this book strives to address what may seem to be more urgent concerns than two of our major entertainment forms, TV and film, but the older and wiser I get, the more concerned and annoyed I become over much of what I see and hear on these two media. Now, I will be the first to admit that I watch entirely too much television despite the fact that I am constantly looking for quality, educational programs dealing with science and nature.

I tune in PBS frequently and have recently found a trove of interesting science "channels" on YouTube. Watching the business news channel has recently claimed a spot in my daily TV viewing ration as I seek to find ways to protect and hopefully grow my meager retirement nest egg. Although there are some differences between the two, for much of this discussion I will lump TV and film into one category referred to as "Hollywood".

In fact, with the advent of streaming, home theater, mega cable and media giants, the line between the two continues to blur as they are now in direct competition in the vast majority of homes with the point and click of a remote control. Whereas when I grew up, we were entertained and informed with just the three major networks and, if lucky, a fourth, upstart PBS (Public Broadcasting).

So without further ado, I will present my complaints, criticisms and finally concerns, some of which should be taken very seriously.

Mumbling

Doesn't this just bug the shit out of you? Actors that are paid good money mumble their lines at the most critical point in a story and you have to screw around with rewind or even put the closed captions on if you want to know what is spoken. What are the directors, editors and producers thinking? Are they even paying attention? Do they not care about their work product? Guess you don't have to worry about believing none of what you hear, the mumblers take care of that.

Darkness

The cousin of mumbling, this complaint seems to be more of a problem with film but TV is not immune to scenes so dark you can barely make out WTH is going on just how some critical scene is actually played out. Perhaps they are trying to keep their electricity bill down and save $ on the budget?

Maybe, but I really think the problem is a result of cheap, unconvincing sets that are best concealed in darkness. When my wife and I start a movie or a TV show and it is dark, we simply thumb down it regardless of the reviews or level of interest. Here again, don't the producers give a hoot?

Herky Jerky

For all the millions spent on film and television productions these days, don't you think they could find a camera person who could hold the camera steady? Or follow the action for more than a few nanoseconds? This is especially bad in action films that are too cheap to choreograph good fight or car chase scenes. I don't care what film, who directs or how many awards, as soon as the action becomes too hard to discern, I deep six the junk.

Fight Scenes

Now here is where TV and Hollywood really fall flat. If the story being told calls for some kind of hand to hand fighting, can somebody, at least one of hundreds of producers, make it even a little realistic? Anyone who has ever seen a real fight, a martial arts tournament, boxing or MMA match, or is simply a person with common sense knows that real fights without padded gloves don't last long, usually just several seconds or a few punches, tops.

However, Hollywood shows blow after blow being exchanged, usually to the face or abdomen with only minor effect when in reality such an encounter would result in putting somebody down after the first or second blow and the way fights are portrayed in TV and film, the losers would be critically injured or likely deceased. Oh, and don't forget the fake sound of a punch landing, the old 60s Batman TV series had it right with the "bop," "biff" and "bams" displayed in written quotes on the screen when a blow supposedly landed.

People become desensitized to the true brutality and danger of actual fighting and many, especially adolescent boys, mimic this behavior and get really hurt during their testosterone-fueled battles for dominance.

Drinking Alcohol

Here is one of my favorites, the way Hollywood portrays drinking, especially spirits. Images of somebody with a bottle of whiskey taking swig after swig or some despondent character pouring glass after glass of straight vodka and slugging it down and still standing?

Wow, a normal human being would be flat on their back if not dead after consuming a full fifth of booze. No wonder college kids drink themselves to death, booze much more than a handful of drinks can be lethal, but they have been conditioned by Hollywood to think that consuming large quantities is no big deal.

Oh and yeah, showing coworkers having a drink in the office after a big victory, you would be so tired in the real world! I am not anti-booze and love a glass of wine or mixed drink now and then but have learned to enjoy alcohol in sips and limited quantities. I have a dear friend who died at age 36 as a result of organ damage caused by alcoholism and I am sure we all know at least one alcoholic. Hollywood, drink responsibly!

Arson

I love it when they show an arsonist pouring gasoline all around inside a building and the perp casually lights a match, tosses it down on the liquid, turns and walks out while the flame burns along the floor following the path of the gasoline, gradually igniting the furniture, drapes etc.

Well, I got news for you and some people, especially fire fighters, chemists and demolitions experts know what I am talking about, the perp in this scenario and many others portrayed in the movies and TV would have their ass blown to kingdom come, in an instant!

Gasoline vapors in even small concentrations are explosive and when trapped in an enclosed space and ignition source is presented, KABOOM! I know of a dilapidated old shed that was blown to bits, almost killing the individual due to ignorance of this scenario.

Fake Sex

Now this one takes the cake and gets my award for "Worst Performance of a Biological Act". Clearly, judging from how hetero sex is portrayed in some of the more risqué (R), mainstream (not XXX Adult) adult oriented movies and series available on the streaming services, the writers, directors and producers know virtually nothing about casual sex hook-ups or for that matter, love making.

What they show is a male-centric coupling with the guy on top in most cases, no prior foreplay, with the happy couple both achieving a rather quiet orgasm at just the same instant! What a joke and how sad for our teenagers to get some of their notions about the subject from this ridiculous interpretation. What is wrong with this portrayal? Just about everything. Where to begin?

First, simultaneous orgasm is pretty rare when and if the woman even gets there during intercourse. That's right guys, women rarely if ever come during screwing, you gotta go down on them, use your finger, tongue or some other imaginative method to please them. They need more time, more foreplay and maybe even a little romance and seduction, not like us "bull in the rut" males.

Oh, and when it occurs, orgasm is a noisy affair, I guess yelling "oh baby, that's it, right there" loudly over and over again must be too gross or illegal or primitive or something. And don't you just love having sex with all your clothes on? Hollywood does.

Here's my last comment for now and listen up Gen X and Boomer dudes, you better start hitting the weights because Gen Z and Millennials are showing us how to do it right, the guy reaches around the gals behind and hoists her up, somehow inserts his dick and proceeds to hump away by tossing her up and down. I'll just bet there are a few injured penises showing up in ERs if much of this is going down. Careful dudes, this is football player only territory.

Fake Gun Violence

Other than creating false stereotypes and taking the pleasure out of perhaps the most enjoyable human activity, sex, Hollywood "Fake Sex" doesn't do all that much harm. But still, buyer beware and believe half of what you see or better yet, none of what you see.

However, Hollywood gun violence is another story entirely and this problem goes all the way back to the early days of film and TV. Let me be clear on this, I am mainly talking about the USA, by far the most gun happy, armed to the teeth, gun death capitol on the planet.

Why is this? We aren't genetically more violent and murderous than the rest of humanity, we represent the most diverse cultural mix, along with the majority being god fearing, plus a set of laws and plenty of police to thwart murder and mayhem. And I don't see the "well-regulated militia protecting the security of our free state," our excuse for the huge numbers of guns saturating American society.

Here's why. Hollywood has evolved into a preoccupation of killing with guns which has become a normalized cultural phenomenon as a result of a hundred years of entertainment media shoot 'em up saturation!

Back in the day, Humphrey Bogart carried a small handgun and maybe shot one or two bad guys all day long. No blood, no camera dwelling on the carnage. Nowadays, a typical cops and robbers flick has multiple scenes with thousands of rounds discharged from military assault weapons and depending on the producers and who the good guys are, hardly any fatalities at all occur (unreal) while in reality many dozens will have been killed. Go figure.

And when somebody gets shot, they just keep on going. Must be superhuman. Makes one think that getting shot isn't all that bad. This is especially problematic for youth and young adults, especially males, most of whom have marginal critical reasoning skills at best. Hollywood has crafted an imaginary world of good guys vs bad guys where the heroes are dispatching evil doers by the dozens with guns.

Far worse than this is the realm of video games wherein the gamer is actively engaged in shooting hundreds of enemies and the enhanced video/sensory quality of modern computer games creates an intense and powerful "learning" environment for engaging in killing.

But that is another story. Bottom line? Hollywood, with the backing of the NRA, has over the decades so saturated entertainment with gun violence that it has become culturally engrained in America and has desensitized society, primarily young and middle-aged white males, to the use of guns as an acceptable means of acting out aggression and frustration.

Fake News

This isn't what you might think, it's not an endorsement of Trump's delusional, paranoid ideation, however, I will give him credit for popularizing the term, one of very few useful products of his fake presidency. I feel like the early Greek philosopher Diogenes the Cynic must have felt when asked why he went about with a lamp in the daylight, his reply being 'I am searching for an honest man.'

My dilemma is the search for an honest, unbiased, informative, news program or, god forbid, unbiased, objective network. As a citizen of Earth, I would like to know, in fact need to know what of significance is going on around the world, be it politics, science, environment and even the arts. Not so much sports, although this has come to play a dominant role in the news.

Unfortunately, the news has become commercialized, a battle for advertising dollars, thus ratings and the quest for ad revenue has morphed network, cable and even YouTube news into an entertainment venue.

Apparently, the producers think we can't take our news straight so they need to water it down, dumb it down and keep repeating the same "headlines" over and over until we become numb to the impact of all the suffering in the world. News networks report what "tests" as popular, what they think will draw viewers, not what the public really should know about.

Global news agencies such as API, UPI and Reuters are wasting their time as far as I can tell. CNN started out on the right foot but it too has become biased, like FOX and MSNBC and that is alright but don't call it news, rather call their programming opinionated reporting or commentary. I grew up watching Walter Cronkite on the evening news with my dad and this is a tradition I have maintained ever since Dad's death in 1974 but the quality, accuracy and thoroughness of the reporting has since become a big disappointment.

Sadly, we remain under-informed and for the most part mis-informed and the News media is responsible for failing to get the facts out so that we can at least make an effort to right the wrongs in the world! Oh, I should not forget to mention that Big Pharma owns and controls the network news!

Reality TV

What did PT Barnum say? 'There's a sucker born every minute.' Well, I contend he way underestimated that total, more like a thousand or ten thousand or whatever number represents 95% of how many humans are born everyday period.

Name a topic or a genre and there is at least one show and probably dozens dealing with the subject. From house flippers to house hunters, from treasure hunters to gold miners, from police stories to court TV. From most talented to most eligible. From chopped cooking champions to worst chef. From six-pack abs in 30 days to pimple poppers.

They're all fake! Be entertained if you like but don't be deceived, all so-called reality TV is bull. The channels that purport to deal with history and discoveries are perhaps the most embellished of all so let the viewer beware!

Passive Viewing

Whether we know it or not and whether we like it or not, virtually all Hollywood product is, with the exception of a few children's shows and *Jeopardy*, 100% passive entertainment. Either willingly and aware, or unconsciously, we open and expose our brains to whatever content and message is being presented, or should I call it downloaded.

That's right, each day's viewing pours thousands of bits of information, good or bad, true or false, straight to our CPU and after that, who knows? All we can say is in some way much of this "information" is processed and it is impossible to say whether the net outcomes will be beneficial or harmful. Depending on what we expose ourselves to, in most cases, we will be intellectually harmed by some of what we view and helped by very little of the rest.

However, since most of the process is passive, very little "beneficial" learning occurs. Hollywood and its investors may argue that they don't promise learning but rather, just entertainment. OK then, Caveat Emptor!

Couch Potatoism

Passive/involuntary deleterious effect of passive learning was discussed above and it is perhaps the most worrisome outcome of consuming Hollywood media be it TV or film. It is an absolute fact that no matter what we watch, learning is occurring involuntarily and at a subliminal (subconscious) level. Even when we are actively engaged and our intellectual filters are on, stuff is still fed to our brains and we have little or no control over this process.

Advertisers especially know this and manipulate the process to sell products using highly seductive, irresistible, multi-exposure commercials cleverly targeted to specific audiences. So what, you may say, that is the price of all the "free" entertainment, news and, in general staying culturally connected and up to date with the rest of the world.

OK, admittedly there is a modicum of value in terms of entertainment and a teense of worthwhile information. But the vast majority is pablum and most of us are putty in the hands of the entertainment media moguls and their sponsors. We have been conditioned since childhood to seek our entertainment passively, sitting on a couch or in a movie theater or at a game console.

In moderation, this may not be so bad but honestly, it is becoming ever harder to moderate our addiction to TV and the movies. Many if not most of us have boring, repetitive jobs, long hours and at the end of the day too little time or energy for hands-on recreation or picking up a book.

OMG! The ugliest of all outcomes is the ever increasing violent country we live in, particularly mass shootings and death by cop, largely resulting from mainstreaming of violence in so much of our Hollywood entertainment from a very young age, combined with the fact that many of us are unable to control the unconscious absorption and passive learning of extremely violent behaviors, nor are we able to control resultant impulses.

Besides, there are six guns for each man, woman and child, and anybody, I mean **anybody**, can get one!

Fake Hollywood, so What?

First of all, it would be hard to deny that the influence of Hollywood on the individual, and society in general is profound and out of control. Additionally, there is a minimal emphasis on education, arts and culture, most of what is produced for our viewing is idiotic fluff and violence.

Sadly, the vast majority of us are unable to filter out the crap and violence, the net result of Hollywood's output being deleterious to society via a process of distracting and stupefying a majority of undisciplined minds. You and me, Jack. Hollywood represents the epitome of free enterprise and thus greed so are we to trust the motives of the moguls and media giants?

I think not since in almost all cases the product is determined by the potential to earn profit and not some higher artistic or intellectual standard. To some extent even educational TV (PBS) is beholden to the almighty dollar since the Republican controlled Congresses have whittled away public funding.

Furthermore, Hollywood serves to distract the masses and that is just what the 1% and political power brokers require in order to maintain control. Distract society from the real situation facing our nation and the human race in general. That may not be so bad if they set about to solve the problems facing humanity, but they don't! Karl Marx's famous quote is especially relevant here, indeed Hollywood is "the opium of the masses"!

Chapter 5
Feeling Good:
The Prime Directive

That's right, feeling good is the most important emotional and physical state, and should be the major undertaking for us all! Seems quite obvious and at the same time excessively self-centered. Well, in a sense it is but the desire to feel good is proper and completely consistent with our biology and, in fact, is necessary if we are to be of much use to society and able to live a purposeful life.

To a certain degree we have lost touch with our survival instinct as an outcome of the development of abstract thinking and thousands of years of a relatively secure and unnatural lifestyle. For the most part, we don't wake up every day completely focused on gathering food, avoiding predation and perhaps even battling other humans to the death.

It would seem that most people, even 3rd world residents, assume personal continuity from day to day and go about the business of daily living, taking life's hard knocks and successes in stride, never fully or at least adequately focused on nurturing the self, be it body, mind or spirit. Subsequently, there are several serious consequences for the individual and society as well.

I have come to conclude that first and foremost we are emotional creatures and secondly, we are thinking (I won't say rational) beings. The Limbic system, which controls emotions, memories and arousal, and constitutes our "survival instinct" evolved well before our early ancestor's brains developed abstract thinking ability, via the cerebral cortex.

As a result, we are wired in a way that emotional states and moods both stimulate and permeate our thoughts. This is partly done via the Limbic system's production of hormones, largely beyond conscious control and the resultant impulses and emotional states underlying most thoughts.

Herein lies the rub, what may once have been a threat to our survival stimulating the fight-or-flight response, may now simply be competition for a parking space and the resultant secretion of adrenaline is way out of proportion to the situation. Or watching a tear jerker movie or reading a sad novel can move us to weeping and sorrow.

My point is that emotions and impulses bubble up moment to moment, mostly out of conscious control and seriously affect, if not totally control, our lives. And perhaps more importantly, these waves of emotion and impulses trigger, influence and even overwhelm our thought processes and ability to act rationally. Oftentimes the resultant state is that of fear, anxiety, confusion and inappropriate action. Suffering.

Another major way physiology dominates our thoughts, moods and deeds is through our state of health/sickness and innumerable associated aches and pains. Try feeling upbeat when you have a pounding headache or nauseous with the stomach flu. Not possible. Or you have a crippling, chronic disease such as arthritis or MS.

There are hundreds if not thousands of illnesses and diseases that plague humanity and these conditions dominate our emotional states and thus thought processes while symptoms are manifest and this results in negative mental states ranging from anxiety, to sadness, to depression and outright despair.

Sadly, these resultant negative mental states overwhelm rational thought processes and often engender desperate acts such as angry acting out, hostile speech, self-harm, violence toward others and even suicide.

We can clearly see that considerable suffering comprises the human experience as does the capacity for much joy, sometimes under the most trying circumstances. What is being suggested here is that our "lizard brain" and state of health strongly affect and in most cases control our thoughts and actions, leading to personal and cultural disorder and chaos.

Due to the distractions of "civilized" lifestyles and widespread poor health caused by poor diet, we have lost touch with our true nature due to the inability to take care of ourselves. We have lost touch with our animal nature, our survival instinct and thus lost focus and the ability to take the steps necessary to feel good.

The contention here is that feeling good is our prime directive and everything flows from how well we do at nurturing the self. I am saying that 'taking care of number one' needs to be our primary focus in life and that does not mean one should be a self-obsessed narcissist. Taking care of oneself no longer is instinctive and seemingly is not taught in the home or in schools. It should be.

In order to have a civil society of a majority of healthy, emotionally stable, contributing members, we need to teach and model for our children the skills for living, not just the three Rs, and by that I mean, healthy eating, emotional sensitivity to both self and other, exercise, impulse control and critical thinking skills.

Ultimately, it is OK to love the self and in fact, is necessary because love is the precursor for empathy, compassion and charity.

Chapter 6
You Really Are What You Eat!

Unless you live in a cave or on a remote mountaintop in the Himalayas, you have at some point heard or read the phrase used to title this chapter. It has been around in some form or other for a long time and for very good reason as I will try to persuade. Perhaps the oldest known use of the phrase was by Jean Anthelme Brillat-Savarin, who, in 1826, wrote, *Tell me what you eat and I will tell you what you are.*

Then several decades later in 1863 the German philosopher Ludwig Andreas Feuerbach, elaborated further on the concept in his essay *Spiritualism and Materialism*, by writing, *A man is what he eats.* (Try and ignore the sexism.) Too bad he didn't consider women as equals but he did get it right about food!

Despite the early origins of the idea, the most famous version which is primarily responsible for its continued use today is that of English nutritionist Victor Lindlahr who in the 1920s said 'Ninety percent of the diseases known to man are caused by cheap foodstuffs, "you are what you eat".'

Later, in 1942 he crystalized this conviction into a relatively popular book, *You Are What You Eat.* In this book, Lindlahr also coined another phrase "food is medicine" and that notion that is still floating around. I and anyone else who cares about their health and physical well-being owe a debt of gratitude to the aforementioned philosopher nutritionists for advancing one of the most critical of the "commandments for living".

Since the purpose of this book is to remind humanity of the laws of nature, our responsibilities as bio-sentient beings as well as rant, rave and laugh a little at our folly, I include a discussion of the importance of eating since it is the most critical biological activity that seems to be understood the least and that includes by the medical profession, nutritionists, Big Pharma and last but not least, the food "industry".

A little unsettling when you think about it that purveying our food has become a factory activity resulting in billions of tons of artificial, chemical laden products half of which are wasteful packaging!

Our species, if you include our early ancestors, has been around for several million years, has been evolving and perfecting a precise combination of genetic material that resulted in a highly intelligent, agile and successful animal that was, unlike all other species, capable of guaranteeing its survival and advancing its dominion over the entire planet.

This gradual process was accomplished by eating a mostly raw, vegan diet at least up until several hundred thousand years ago, and then on a 100% natural omnivorous diet. With the discovery of fire and cooking along with eating cooked grains within the last 100,000 years or so, we began to stray from our species specific diet but still subsisted on a natural diet, if not progressively more unbalanced, i.e., meat, grain and cooking focused.

With these most recent developments, we solved the problem of caloric shortage and lack of fat, a certain amount of which is necessary for brain development but we gradually and drastically reduced the quantities of vitamins, minerals and critical enzymes available primarily in raw fruits and veggies.

Based on the discussion so far which is driven and supported by anthropological and archaeological evidence, (in my opinion) some rules for optimal human diet include, as well as important things to avoid, are as follows:

1. We are by design primarily herbivores fructivores like our cousins, the Great Apes.
2. We have the teeth and digestive tract designed for raw fruits, nuts and green plants.
3. Heat/cooking destroys essential nutrients, especially vitamins and enzymes.
4. We do not have the short digestive tract of a carnivore.
5. Meat putrefies in our long digestive tract.
6. We are not grain eaters by design, especially cooked.
7. Domesticated animal flesh, except fish, is high in artery clogging cholesterol.
8. Refined grains, i.e., flours, are broken down into sugar, the most harmful of all "edibles" when digested.

As can be seen above, the modern diet of homo sapiens, including the 1st, 2nd and 3rd worlds, has strayed from our species specific diet and placed TOO heavy emphasis on high-fat, high-carb, high-protein diets that lead to heart disease, diabetes and cancer, to name a few.

One could argue that we live longer than in pre and even early historic times and I believe this is largely due to starvation avoidance and disease prevention via improved sanitation but not improved nutrition. If not even one of the above eight points resonates with you, the following rationale hopefully will.

First, allow me to backtrack a bit. What is meant by the statement 'you are what you eat?' Clearly it is not meant literally, which would be absurd and some choose to take that meaning and thus dismiss the point of the statement entirely, which is that there is a direct relationship with what you eat and the constitution of your body. So, if not meant to be taken literally, what then shall we make of the statement?

Perhaps an analogy would be helpful. Most humans think of and treat their bodies like an incinerator, aka trash burner, which will burn just about any organic, plant, animal or "food" product and it will produce heat. The same applies to the food they eat. If the body will process it (burn) and there is no immediate, untoward consequence and the taste is pleasant, then it is suitable food.

The problem here is that the effects, whether beneficial or deleterious, of what we put in our gut are gradual. So in most cases, we cannot tell which foods are beneficial and which deleterious. Furthermore, with advances in science and biology over the last several hundred years we have learned that our bodies are constantly repairing damaged tissue, rebuilding organs and replacing dead cells with new ones and this requires the proper nutrients, not just fuel for the incinerator.

In fact, nutritional science and subsequently the FDA has it worked out to Percentage Daily Value (% DV) for virtually anything sold as food so it is reasonably well known what is required to repair and rebuild cells in the body.

Here's the rub, though. First of all, most of us don't take seriously the fact that precise nutrients in proper quantities are required to sustain and grow the human body. Does anybody actually keep a tally of their % DV through the day? And if you really cared, how would you account for fresh, non-packaged foods without labels?

Secondly, even if one were to track and actually consume 100% DV of all the "necessary" food groups, it remains to be seen just how healthy that individual would be though I suspect they would be considerably better off than the person on the standard American diet (SAD) consisting mostly of fast foods, soft drinks, sweets and too much meat.

If we look closely at the animal kingdom, we see that virtually all creatures have a specific diet that, barring starvation, is never varied. Hundreds of thousands and even millions of years of eating specific foods have shaped each species and that is no different for us. We have evolved highly sophisticated, advanced physiologies eating specific foods and logic follows that in order to thrive we must adhere to our species specific diet.

Clearly, we have not and this is evidenced by the vast numbers of illnesses and diseases that plague mankind. Add to this extensive suffering and unhealthy human condition the proliferation of a vast chemical industry producing stimulants (medicines) that suppress symptoms and block the body's pain signals meant to warn us of improper conditions, i.e., wrong eating, and we can clearly see that what we are and what we are becoming is absolutely a result of what we eat.

It seems clear after examining in some detail the old adage "you are what you eat" (YAWYE) that our survival, health and vitality are a direct result of the types of foods we eat and though the statement is a somewhat vague generalization, it should form the foundation of each individual's food choices as well as prompt a more careful analysis by medical and nutritional science which in my opinion has not been done, resulting in what now constitutes a total misunderstanding of what the optimal human diet is.

I do not see standards for truly healthy eating with dietary recommendations in the doctor's office, media or public information realm. Combine this with a profit-based food industry producing and flooding the grocery world with packaged products high in salt, sugar and fat, devoid of nutrients, seductively marketed and we have the resultant, obese, unhealthy society we see today.

Furthermore, while the medical establishment probably agrees, at least in part with YAWYE, by and large they fail to adequately incorporate diet and nutrition in the practice of medicine. This applies to both prevention of sickness and disease as well as healing. It doesn't take a rocket scientist to see this failure and I certainly qualify as a non-rocket scientist and in that spirit have undertaken a lifelong search for the ideal diet, true health, vitality and disease-free living and will discuss my findings in a subsequent chapter.

Chapter 7
It's All About Me

Two chapters back, I wrote about the importance of taking care of number one, that feeling good is a prime directive for each of us, but will now attempt to put this basic human need in clearer perspective and explain as well as provide insights on how to correct the pandemic of narcissism and greed that exists in the world today.

We have already established the biological necessity of taking care of number one as it is a precursor to survival of the species. I have also promoted the absolute importance of feeling good in order to carry out our responsibilities as global citizens in an effective, humane manner. The problem is that in a significant number of us the needs of the individual are manifested in the form of out-of-control egotism which, when combined with access to wealth and political power, has caused chaos and suffering as far back as one cares to examine the historical record.

With the evolution of our big brains over the eons, nature produced and evolution selected intelligence and the ability to think, to conceptualize via abstraction and therefore modify aspects of the environment which resulted in a highly successful species. And somewhere along the way, within the depths of our very large brains, mostly likely within the frontal cortex, the light of consciousness blinked on.

What an amazing development, the universe of inanimate matter had woken up to its own existence with the rise of sentient beings truly aware of themselves and the world around them.

However, it would seem this miraculous development was not without cost. Homo sapiens were no longer governed by instinct, but rather had been endowed with the ability to defy natural law, and ultimately make decisions and act in ways that were not necessarily in the best interest of themselves or their tribe, and more importantly, not consistent with nature's mandates.

With the rise of abstract thinking, the balance of nature had been tipped disproportionately in favor of our species. We no longer survived like virtually all other species by hunting/gathering. We developed artificial means of guaranteeing food supplies with the advent of agriculture and domestication of animals for food.

For millennia, this was not a problem but eventually these highly efficient means of guaranteeing food supplies led to the population boom of our species. We developed non-sustainable farming via slash and burn as well as over fishing with the development of large nets. We were on our way to overcrowding the Earth's habitable zone and exhausting soils and the supply of game animals.

As a group, our species was very clever in developing means of survival but seemingly never once considered the effect our methods had on the environment or other living creatures we share it with.

Why is this? Certainly we can see that there are plenty of ways to farm, fish and hunt that do not decimate the environment and its inhabitants. The same is true for industry and the mass production of tools, shelters, vehicles and all the myriad gizmos and gadgets we crave but have little purpose or biological advantage.

It is quite clear that we are very clever and capable of making things, many if not most of which are without any direct benefit to the well-being or advancement of our species. All along the path of the rise of civilization we have forged ahead, motivated initially by survival but eventually by self-interest and greed (capitalism) with nary a consideration given to the possible consequences of our actions.

Our activities on the home planet have in just over 200 years since the industrial revolution put in motion climatological changes, i.e., rapid planetary warming that threatens our very existence and that of numerous other species of plants and animals on both land and sea. Believe me, Earth doesn't give a shit. It has witnessed quite of few minor and several mass extinction events. But not so unique and ironic as the suicide by greenhouse effect that we have so carelessly set in motion. So are we so smart?

It would appear that while we are very clever, very "intelligent tool makers," the broader effects of our activities on the environment and ecosystems demonstrate that we are shortsighted, excessively self-centered and unable to comprehend the big picture. Ergo, I submit that as a whole, we are not very wise and nor are we sufficiently endowed with common sense.

However, what we definitely are is greedy and lacking in "awareness". As much as we are gifted with abstract thinking capability, and a degree of mathematical and mechanical intelligence, it would seem the majority of humankind are unduly influenced and primarily controlled by primal "instincts" and baser emotions of greed and self-aggrandizement.

Unfortunately, we are not naturally endowed with common sense and critical or wholistic thinking, at least not on a large enough scale to make a difference. I am not a Christian but am fond of a famous quote attributed to Jesus, Luke 23:34 'Father forgive them for they know not what they do' and I assume that is meant to apply to those who crucified him, but I, and I am sure many others, see the broader applicability to the human condition.

Amazingly, 500 years before the time of Christ, Buddha identified the three causes of suffering as greed (craving), hatred (anger) and delusion (ignorance) and offered a way to transcend it but unfortunately, over 2600 years later too few have gotten the message.

It would seem unavoidable if we honestly assess the state of affairs of humanity and what we have done and continue to do to other living things and to the Earth in general, that we are seriously flawed as a species.

In fact, we have identified emotional and mental diseases and defects galore that are widespread, including depression, suicide, neurosis, schizophrenia, bipolar disorder, sociopathology, psychopathology, and narcissistic personality disorder.

Amazingly, the USA elected an individual as president, Donald Trump, who unapologetically displayed and manifested for the world to see, most disturbing behaviors and warped thinking, a textbook case of a sociopath with narcissistic personality disorder.

And to think that he is worshipped by nearly 40% of the US voting public, what a mind-boggling and frightening situation! And Trump is just a somewhat tepid example of the mad, evil, fascists, tyrants and conquerors that have come down through the ages and even now hold sway in our time (Putin, Kim Jong-un and Xi Jinping). How have we tolerated these individuals? How have we even followed them and abided by their evil? What is wrong with "US"?

Thankfully, the scourge of the Hitler and the Nazis was defeated but white supremacy and antisemitism are still rampant around the world.

I don't know man, seems I am killing my own buzz with this discussion. But shit, what the hell are WE going to do about it? Is there anything we can do? We are, as far as can be known for sure, nature's only great experiment with the evolution of sentience, language, consciousness and the ability to do science.

That is simply astonishing when you think about it. We are unraveling the secrets of creation and yet we can't get our own house in order and seem to be on the road to extinction, what a great shame that would be. We are contemplating the exploration of the galaxy, venturing forth to the stars, my god, people, let's get our act together!

The problem is, despite the evolution of sentience, consciousness and abstract thinking, too many of us are overly influenced by our primal desires and emotions which to some extent direct our thoughts and actions.

Unfortunately, in the majority of us the executive function of the brain, the conscience, and the more noble emotions such as compassion and empathy, as well as on the intelligence side, insight and awareness, are emergent qualities of the human brain and have not manifested in a sufficient percentage of the population to have positively affected the course of history.

Compounding the problems and lack of higher intellectual functioning just cited, we appear to be and still act as tribal societies. The strongest, loudest, boldest most extroverted emerge as leaders, not necessarily the most intelligent, compassionate and experienced and this is evident in 1st, 2nd and 3rd world countries.

Down through the ages we have seen this scenario repeated and shockingly and to the great disdain of women and men of compassion, intelligence and conscience, most recently with the election of Donald Trump as the President of the USA.

He is a textbook narcissist, sociopath, racist, misogynist, unapologetic liar and bully. A perfect example of the phenomenon of the "cult of personality," this fascist leaning, anti-politician was able to sway over 70 million so-called educated, religious, moral citizens by employing undisguised, crude, ingratiation tactics and appealing to voters' fears, bigotry, ignorance of the issues and disillusionment with Washington politics as usual.

His aberrant presidency, culminating in the Big Lie delusion and January 6 Insurrection have irreparably divided the "United" States and fomented the early stages of the 2nd civil war.

Well, based on the complete lack of shared philosophy, values and understanding of the Constitution, it is for the best that red and blue states, counties and cities go their own way, as I have argued in a previous chapter.

The crux of the problem is the fact that greed, anger and delusion are powerful, bedrock, highly dominant drives, the first two being a manifestation of survival mechanisms. Unfortunately, the higher intellectual functions of insight and impulse control have not evolved sufficiently in most humans to monitor and control them.

To our detriment, this is the case in many, if not most individuals and society as a whole, and it would seem that the pace of the forces of evolution with respect to the human brain are at best way too slow, if existent at all, with respect to rewiring our species from primitive primates to "thinking" homo sapiens. Add to this scenario the fact that like most other predatory species, there is the tendency toward dominance by brute force and that seems to still be an existential problem for us.

Despite the fact that our tech-centered cultures are driven by intelligence, creative thinking and cooperation, rulers and politicians more often than not gain power by coercive, forceful means and are with few exceptions egocentric, brash, violent bullies.

While it is unknown just how many humans are emotion and impulse dominant versus how many are rational, social, intellectual creatures, there always have been, are now, and continue to be sufficient numbers of cavemen in suits and ties that force their way to the top leadership positions and cause irreparable harm to their fellow humans and all of nature.

Have you heard or do you remember the brilliant, insightful song, *I, Me, Mine*, by the Beatles? Where George laments our egocentric preoccupation with I and Me and Mine? All through the day and night by just about everyone conflicted with this unmitigated self absorption. The noble thing to do is to resist this narcissism by studying the self as the Beatles so wisely advised!

Chapter 8
The Secret of True Health Revealed

If I do one thing for humanity before I leave this life, it is to impress upon a significant number of people (I know, what is significant?) especially those who are suffering from disease and feeling helpless and hopeless, or those who just want to attain a higher level of functioning and experience a truly vital body free from sickness and disease, what I have learned in over 50 years of personal dietary experimentation: and that is a path to real health and superior vitality.

Of course, what I will discuss in this chapter is my opinion based on actual affliction with various illnesses and disease with subsequent experimentation on numerous diets and detoxes in attempt to promote healing and avoidance of future sickness.

I won't be surprised if an attempt is made to either censor my claims and opinions on health by the big kahuna of book selling and self-publishing, or social media, whom I think you all may know very well. But I assure you, I have no ulterior motives other than to pass along the secret to true health as it has been revealed to me and I assure you it is a quantum leap from what medical science believes exists and promotes as "healthy".

Furthermore, anything I discuss here is not meant to be construed as medical advice and I am in no way suggesting anyone veer from the advice of their doctor.

So, what am I getting at? Sticking to the point of this book of no bullshit and cutting to the chase, I will give you my version, a redefinition of sorts, of what being healthy really means. But first allow me to recommend a book I have written and self-published that elaborates in detail what true health is and how to achieve it, entitled *The Raw, Vegan, Alkaline Diet Handbook for Superior Health and Vitality* on Amazon/Kindle, only $8 and $5, respectively.

In a nutshell, the most commonly accepted definition of health is a 'state in which a person has apparent social, mental, and physical well-being and has no illness present.' This is similar to the definition adopted by the WHO and is quite vague. My definition of health goes well beyond that and represents a state that few attain and medical science may take issue with.

In my view, true health means '**never get sick, does not develop disease, has superior vitality, exceptional mental clarity, a persistent positive emotional state and long life**.' In many cases, a newborn comes into the world truly healthy, assuming the mother ingested a modicum of healthy, fresh, plant based foods, avoided drugs and harmful substances.

Fortunately, the placenta is somewhat selective in passing through the best available nutrition to the fetus and avoiding some harmful substances, but not all. However, and sadly, after the baby is born, once it has started on solid food and certainly not much after the mother stops nursing, it is all downhill, at least in terms of health.

Did you ever see an infant with snot drooling from its nose? Probably being fed dairy and/or grain based cereals, both of which are highly acid forming (mucus producing) and not suited to our digestive systems or metabolism and thus the young body is wise enough to attempt to eliminate them via mucus.

In a previous chapter, I attempted to drive home the point that eating right is one of the most important things we do since "you are what you eat" and over millions of years nature has via evolution programmed pretty specific nutritional needs and digestive capabilities into each and every one of us and as such the body either malfunctions (gets sick, dies) or in the least functions far less than it would have had our species specific diet been followed.

That's right friends, nature intended for us to eat certain foods in certain ways and these requirements along with certain restrictions are due to our ancestors adapting over millions of years to the natural environment they evolved in and what was available as food to them was primarily plant based with perhaps some insects and scavenging at fresh kills, although our long digestive tract suggests we are best suited primarily for a plant-based diet.

The critical issue here is that since the discovery of fire and agriculture, we have veered significantly from the mostly raw, vegan, highly alkaline diet we evolved on. As such, in modern homo sapiens we see a raft of ailments and diseases that didn't exist in the distant past nor even 100 years ago, as a consequence of our aberrant diet of cooked, processed, sugary, fatty, animal tissue based diet.

Enough background. The current Covid-19 pandemic graphically illustrates my point, at least in part with regard to what true health really is. I, and I am sure most of us, know somebody or have heard of somebody who was or "seemed" so-called healthy that either died or got really sick from the virus and needed to be hospitalized.

Now those individuals were/are not healthy by my definition! I have heard doctors and health experts come on the TV news and state that "healthy" people are getting sick and dying from Covid, the Delta or Omicron Variant and I wonder how they could have been considered healthy? Just because somebody is not manifesting symptoms at present or for a stretch of time between ailments does not represent actual health.

My contention is that there is a higher threshold of health and vitality to be experienced and I have been fortunate enough to have learned one dietary system that lays out what is required nutritionally to achieve it.

Why me? Not totally sure about that but I suspect it is due to a combination of dissatisfaction with my health as a 21 year young man, curiosity, willingness to do the homework (reading), idealism and finally adequate will power and an experimentation with a wide variety of natural, sometimes extreme vegan diets.

Over a period of 33 years until about age 54 and discovering I had prostate cancer, I read dozens of the most popular, innovative books on natural diet and nutrition, as well as tested many versions of vegetarian, vegan, pescatarian, paleo and fruitarian diets along with performed over 100 detoxes, juices cleanses and fasts.

Up until the cancer diagnosis, I thought I was "pretty healthy" rarely getting "sick" but obviously I was way wrong. The prospects for treatment given me in 2003 by the Urologist, radiation or surgical removal of the prostate with the risk of impotency, were not acceptable so I resolved to redouble my efforts at finding the optimal diet with what I hoped to have healing and rejuvenation capabilities.

By that time, I believed that the ideal diet for mankind consisted of mostly fresh fruits and vegetables, low fat, low sugar, no fried, no processed, low mucus forming and no/low animal based foods. In fact, I was follower and sometimes practitioner of the Mucusless Diet developed by Arnold Ehret in the early 20th century but didn't really understand what in all the food groups caused excess mucus and what that truly represented.

Doing reading on cancer cures on the internet, I happened on the pH Miracle Diet by Robert Young and Eureka, that was it. His research and treatment of sick clients using a highly pH (alkaline) juice cleanse and mostly raw, vegan transition diet resulted in amazing healing and revitalization based on testimonials from his patients and that convinced me to try it.

Subsequently, I went on a 99% raw, vegan, alkaline (RVA) diet and after six months my psa score had dropped and a small tumor on the prostate had disappeared! That was all the proof I needed that I had finally found the key elements of the ideal diet for mankind and began to glimpse what true health could be.

After the detox/transition to a raw, vegan, alkaline (RVA) diet I felt fantastic: senses clearer, lost 20 lbs. of fat, dropped from eight hours of sleep to six, increased physical energy and flexibility, improved libido (I know TMI), mental sharpness unlike before, and a new, positive, joyful outlook on life. Hard to believe right? But I am not BS-ing, no reason to, not selling anything, just trying to get the word out.

As a result of the high pH, RVA detox performed in 2004 and the amazing healing I experienced, I resolved to adopt a mostly RVA diet in conjunction with eliminating stimulants such as coffee and alcohol and after several years of this I began to notice some pretty amazing physical changes along with a major, sustained improvement in my health and vitality.

My need for sleep continued to decrease until it dropped to five hours with more lucid dreams and waking very refreshed. I no longer got the occasional headache. Annual dental checkups and cleanings indicated improvement in the gums with no new cavities.

Also, no longer getting the occasional head cold or flu. Significantly improved flexibility enabled me to do yoga postures I previously was unable to do. Better hand-eye coordination. Seemingly boundless energy when running, biking or even doing manual labor, improved mental clarity and sharpened thought processes. When conversing and writing, words and ideas definitely flowed better.

Overall, I was feeling really good, emotionally in a sublime space along with enhanced compassion and abiding love for all "creation". Essentially, all this occurred over a period of about five years on an average of 95% RVA diet, with what proved to be vastly improved nutrition. Despite growing five years older, I was better in every imaginable regard, completely rejuvenated and revitalized, and at nearly age 60 I felt like I was 30 again and in some ways even better.

In fact, my health was better than it ever was, never sick and cancer in remission, feeling good all the time and along with my overall performance as a person and satisfaction with living, I realized what being healthy truly meant. And that state is attainable by virtually anyone with access to fresh fruits and vegetables and select, low acid nuts and seeds.

Now, finally to the main point. I hope I have described adequately the sequence of events in an average person's journey from sickness to true health. And even if there is some skepticism on behalf of you the reader, which I respect, I would hope that anyone reading this is convinced or at least allows for the possibility that what heretofore has been assumed to be a state of "health" is a disappointment and that the health and wellness status quo is far less than what I and a quite a few other health seekers have learned to be the true potential for the human body.

So here it is, a new definition of health:

'True Health is the whole body condition where we never get sick, do not contract disease (aside from strong chemical exposure, toxin ingestion, radiation etc.), preexisting sickness heals naturally, most chronic diseases mitigate and eventually heal, where mental clarity is exceptional, emotional well-being is enhanced, positive emotions dominate, and individual lifespan is extended well beyond the norm, well into the hundreds, all resultant from a high percentage raw, vegan, alkaline diet.'

So there you have it, a new way of viewing one aspect of the human condition and in a sense a challenge to the medical establishment to break with convention and take a fully natural approach to the problem of sickness and health.

While there may be other natural health and vitality advocates and pioneers, I haven't seen much in the literature and certainly nothing in the MSM (mainstream media) making the bold claims like I am, aside from the benefits of "eating healthy," organics and the occasional new fad or superfood.

I am certain though there are quite a few others that think along similar lines and to those persons congratulations on your accomplishment, insight and courage to pursue a bold new way of living and thriving!

My intent with this discussion is to tell the true story of one person's long journey of discovery with continual dietary experimentation and at the risk of sounding overly dramatic, persistence on a search for true health and ultimate vitality, which I hypothesized was possible when I was 21 years old.

Since the purpose of this book is to call out, debunk, challenge, teach (that's right), offer hope, alternatives, shame into action, and even mourn, I hereby humbly submit my take on a new paradigm for true health and vitality.

Chapter 9
Problems with the News

What is the News? What has it become? What should it be?

After 73 years of which over 60, I have spent watching some version of the TV network news, and sometimes from radio, despite advancements in technology and journalism methodology, instead of becoming more informative, more accurate and useful to the citizenry, the "News" has devolved into a mishmash of shock, hype, sensationalism, sappy stories, mind-numbing drug ads, preoccupation with murder, anti-heroes, focus on tragic loss and suffering, celebrity worship, partisan slanted political reporting, complete departure from journalistic standards and on and on.

In order to keep abreast of current events on a national and global scale, I am afraid the average person and even the newshound have set themselves on a fool's errand. You would think with the proliferation of cable, TV news only networks and media conglomerates and all of that effort and investment dedicated to the News, one would be able to easily (or even with effort) seek out and learn about anything and everything of consequence happening in the country and the world but sadly that is not the case. WTF?

My love/hate affair with watching the news started with my dad, when after a hard day's work as a carpenter, he would kick back, maybe with a cold beer before dinner and watch CBS News with Walter Cronkite, where the reporting was reasonably objective, to the point and made an attempt in 30 minutes to inform the viewer of the most important current events going on in the world and nation.

Upon closing with his signature "and that's the way it is," you could be reasonably sure (I think) you had been updated on the most critical issues of the day. No fluff, no sports, no entertainment, no weeping widows on the set, and most importantly, just reporting. There did not seem to be any hidden agenda or attempt to persuade and entertain such as exists in MSM today.

Back then, the network news was seen as a public service and journalistic standards applied. Since in the 50s and early 60s there were really only 3 VHF networks and upstart PBS, the competition for viewers wasn't anywhere as tight as it is in 2022 so the producers didn't feel they had to "sell" the news using "gotchas," sensationalism and celebrities.

There was a sense of responsibility as a corporate citizen and information outlet to simply keep the public informed by reporting on the leading stories around the nation and the world.

How noble. But, of course, all the news that mattered could not be reported in a half hour or even an hour if you count the local affiliates reporting on state, regional and local matters. Comprehensive news coverage was left to the newspapers and most did a reasonable job of that but now it gets ever harder to find any print news content amidst page after page of ads.

Somewhere along the way things began to change with the advent of cable and the news networks, the first being CNN and back in the day it too did a pretty good job of reporting the news and given its 24-hour format was able to cover much more in greater depth. Not long after, CNN was followed by an increasing number of so-called alternative "news" networks and the competition became more and more fierce.

The major networks found themselves under ever-increasing competition to make a profit and as such, more and more "creative" means were devised to retain viewers, thus advertisers and ultimately profit. Well, that was the beginning of the end for useful, factual news content.

Since the process of making the news profitable entailed competing with numerous cable entertainment channels in the time slot, apparently MSM news producers made the decision to make it more "entertaining" and that was the beginning of the end. I believe this devolution began back in the late 70s and since then there has been progressively less actual news content and we are left today with the disappointing variety shows that pose as news.

The demise of true journalistic reporting by TV news organizations is a huge disappointment for several reasons, at least for boomers and Gen Xr's. It would seem that Millennials and Gen Z get their news, if they get it at all, via social media and cell phone apps and any chance of objectivity there is remote since information and truth are liberally manipulated and tailored for specific audiences by sophisticated algorithms designed to boost advertising, sales and subscribers.

Even scarier is the fact that the younger generations are relying on "influencers" with very little academic or journalistic credibility, for staying informed, if you want to call it that.

So if we acknowledge that TV and MSM (mainstream media) is down the toilet, it is probably the case that social media, YouTube, Facebook, Twitter, TikTok, Instagram, YouTube and all the apps that purport to report on current events are even worse and any of US who care about the state of the nation and the globe are pretty much screwed since it is virtually impossible to get a truthful, timely, accurate fix on what is going on and consequently our ability to act in earnest to address problems is hamstrung.

So as I see it the lack of comprehensive, factual news reporting on all outlets and media to all generations is an existential threat to society. It is next to impossible for individuals and the populace to accurately assess and address problems when we can't trust the reporting in an attempt to form a fact-based understanding of the true state of human affairs.

Allow me to cite some of my concerns and complaints with the "News". The root word of "News" is "new" and what we are served by the media contains just a small percentage of new information and rather offers an ad-nauseam, overdose and rehash of what are perceived to be the "big stories," those that seem to get the ratings and are shoved down our gullets until we are mind-numbed and desensitized to the seriousness of the given situation.

The next problem I see with the news is that, across the board, it is inconsistently reported, i.e., some stories dominating the airtime based on a perceived ratings benefit while others have far too little or no time at all despite the true importance and potential benefit to the viewer. As such, so many important issues never, never see the light of day, especially surrounding the greatest issue of our time and perhaps history, global warming! Other problems include:

- Entertainment "News," is just useless fluff and should be replaced with current events pertaining to environment, politics, weather science, culture, etc.
- Preoccupation with ratings, murders, and anything with shock value.
- Sports. Why is this on the mainstream news? Go to ESPN!
- Silliness. Anchors and reporters giggling and cracking jokes seem to think they are comedians, get real.
- Chit-chat. Just read the news and stop the gabbing!
- Abandonment of the "who, what, when, where, why" standard of reporting.

Seems a little harsh? Well, we live in precarious times and those of us who care about the well-being of humanity and the planet need to be informed in real time about what is going on in society, politics, war, education, science and the environment so that we can take action. It seems that based on what is being reported on virtually all formats, the news media have lost touch with the purpose of their being.

Can anything be done to bring objective reporting back and, in fact, elevate the news to a high journalistic standard?

Lacking an outcry from sophisticated, intelligent viewers along with a broad boycott of the current bullshit offering across the current TV news spectrum, I doubt it. Lacking an epiphany in MSM newsrooms or should I say boardrooms regarding the serious issues facing humanity and the critical need to truly inform and educate, I doubt it. Lacking adequate funding for PBS to mount a broader, more headline oriented, global news initiative and along with less overly detailed human interest reporting, I doubt it.

This discussion of the decline of the news won't be complete without mention of the elephant in the room, wait for it, "Fake News". The irony here is that Trump and his legions of deluded followers who cry "fake news," along with the far-right propaganda mouthpiece Fox, are the "fakest" of them all.

And the far right news outlets aren't alone, of course there is Facebook, the last format you want to get news from and I would charge the left of center CNN and MSNB frequent manipulation of the facts on occasion as a means placating their sponsors and promoting their liberal agenda. They are all, for the most part, editorializing, not reporting and sadly, most of their viewers are seemingly not smart enough to know the difference.

And the problem is exacerbated by the fact that there is no good news organization in MSM or anywhere else for that matter as far as I can tell!

Part of the dilemma is that double-edge sword, the First Amendment with its provision for free speech and free press. There is no constitutional mandate for speaking truthfully or in the case of the press, reporting factually, and combine the legal right to "lie" with the unavoidable truth that a large part of the populace are ignorant, poorly educated, easily duped, unable to discern fact from fiction even when it smacks them in the face (e.g., Big Lie, Birthers) and I am referring to all the Trumpers and MAGAs and a fair number of the center and left, and the result is a massive stir-pot of confusion, anger, violence and lack of right thinking and action for the good of society.

So what can be done about this very significant problem? I hate to say "nothing" but things have gotten so far out of hand that it is unlikely that anything can be done.

But "we" have to start somewhere and I would call on the media moguls to search their conscience and take their eyes off the profit margin and promoting their own political, religious agendas and actually start reporting newsworthy world and national events without bias so that there is at least a chance for society to see the world as it truly is and begin to work toward resolution of the problems that threaten our very existence starting with global warming, followed closely by political violence, fascism, overpopulation, environmental degradation and threat of nuclear warfare.

Somebody, some MSM CEO, some board of directors will have to take the lead and with a declaration of "return to truth and highest standards of journalism" begin in a very public way, reporting broadly, truthfully and without bias or preoccupation with profit, to tell the "whole truth, nothing but the truth, so help you god". Or whatever higher power they report to.

Chapter 10
Understanding the Self

This is, without a doubt, the most important question facing all of us, at least those of us who ponder existence and actually attempt to utilize our amazing brains for the purpose of which they are intended by nature. Or if not intended, at least equipped to tackle.

That is, I believe, to animate the material universe, to bring character, sentience and a unique form of creativity to a google of particles behaving in somewhat prescribed, rote, predictable fashion. Aspire to utilize the gift of consciousness many are endowed with and most are capable by of manifesting and advancing the state of creation, and I mean this not in the biblical sense, by celebrating and perfecting awakened mind and ultimately evolving into "Gods".

No offense to believers but if we are children of god, are we not then nascent gods? No doubt we humans are arguably the top of the evolutionary heap, at least so far as we can tell and we are presented with an amazing opportunity and responsibility to live up to our potential. As such, part of the point of this chapter is to clarify and promote the notion of taking ownership and responsibility for having intelligence and consciousness, and to do so I believe we must address the question 'Who am I?'

It doesn't matter in what theistic religion or non-dogmatic, atheist, agnostic or rational background you were brought up in addressing the hard question of "who am I" is essential. Let's explore this notion from a variety of perspectives.

At some point after reaching the age of 7, a child is considered by the Roman Catholic Church to have reached the 'age of reason' (I was raised Roman Catholic) and is entitled to receive communion, i.e., directly connect their soul to God. Some evangelical churches hold that a child of seven can make an independent spiritual choice. Amazing!

Now I think that seven may be a little young to understand god and make religious choices, except for the brightest and most precocious and I would postulate it is more like age 13 at the earliest. And calling this brain event "age of reason" is perhaps attributing quite a bit more intellectual ability to a young child than is reasonable or attainable so I would much rather call this stage of intellectual growth and brain maturation the "age of self-awareness".

At this stage, the areas of the brain are developing and billions of neuronal connections are being laid down to the extent that major brain centers, including sensory, attention, emotion, abstract thought, short term/long-term memory, are increasingly cross connected and "communicating," one result being a sense of permanent, separate self.

It is my understanding that over eons of evolution, the survival instincts of the human brain have morphed into a set of behavior patterns which then were selected out and further developed into a combination of hard-wiring and software for emergence of Ego or Self. Memory, perception, awareness and emotion all play a major part in creating this sense of continuity and separateness.

It is apparent to me that evolution has, through genus "Homo," promoted the growth of the brain, with numerous specialty centers foremost among them and unique to the genus, memory, abstract thinking, awareness, all contributing to the emergence of a strong sense of the individual which seemingly resulted in a set of abilities that enabled our species to become increasingly more successful at survival.

However, the rise of the strong individual awareness, when combined with the still dominant "lizard brain" and its primitive emotions of fear, greed and violence more deeply ingrained, made for and still makes a potentially dangerous combination.

It would seem that, and it is unfortunate as well, that the more noble human emotions of love, compassion, morality and generosity are not as deeply ingrained nor are they dominant. It is my opinion that despite our immense intellectual talents, we are still quite primitive, violent and short sighted.

Just look at the state of current global politics and the historical record and we see never ending violence and war that far overshadow our accomplishments in art and science.

So what is my point? Simply this, that most humans are operating under the illusion that they are a separate self, a "me" versus them, that "my" needs are more important than the rest, that "I" am entitled to all I can get, and that "I" will live forever, even after death and that the afterlife is more important than this current existence!

I contend that despite our big brains with their many intellectual abilities; we are failing as a species in that many of us since the dawn of time, throughout our history, have failed to utilize our great potential, have to this day propagated crimes against humanity and nature in general and obviously remain governed by the primitive, violent, emotions.

The dominance of our brutish, selfish, violent tendencies and the failure of more noble, socially conscious, intelligent people to overcome and thwart "evil" in our species has brought us to the brink of extinction, where we remain, since the invention and proliferation of thermonuclear weapons.

While much of this book wrestles directly with the "Big Truth," the fact that we are fucking up, the nature of the self may not at first seem relevant to saving the planet but I say it is. By asking the question "who am I," we open a critical internal dialogue of self-examination that is a prerequisite for the development of awareness, a set of ideals, moral standards and right actions.

In fact, in order to overcome our brutish nature and tendency toward greed and violence, the brain must be taught to control our primitive impulses, and religion, childhood education and socialization are not enough.

Sometime upon attaining the "age of awareness" some of us (hopefully many) may have a spontaneous experience, perhaps somewhat dissociative, of not knowing "who we are". For me, it was looking in the mirror one day around age 11 or so and seeing a young person staring back and wondering "who is that," "is that me" and that led ultimately to the question "who am I"?

I am not sure what this brain event is called and how many experience it but I consider it fortuitous and it or something like it is necessary to initiate the search for "personal identity" and ultimately the search for and realization of our *true nature*.

I postulate that this process is the all-important, necessary step in individual and species wide human evolution, to have a kind of deep realization, through awareness and focused mindfulness wherein we learn to utilize our great brains and gain control over the caveman within each of us.

The father of Western Philosophy, the brilliant Greek Socrates, is attributed to have stated 'Man, know thyself,' and I believe no greater advice has ever been given. Regardless of whether you believe you have a soul or not, whether you believe in god or not, your life is quite meaningless without questioning and attempting to understand the nature of your being.

That may not be the reason consciousness evolved in us but it is the most obvious critical step in embracing and fully realizing the intellectual gifts we have inherited.

Let me say right off that deep awareness is not a given and the search for one's true self is not an automatic aspect of the human condition, although I believe most of us are provided many internal and external cues that prompt us to introspection.

Most instances of suffering and trauma motivate us to question the cause or reason for our pain and believe it or not, this presents an opportunity. It opens the door to introspection and the inevitable question "why me"? In attempting to unravel the "why," invariably the notion of a "me" is exposed to examination and the door to insight is cracked open.

Clearly there is suffering, sensations of pain and negative emotions arise, but who, what or where is the "me," that is suffering?

I challenge anyone, atheist or believer alike, to locate this self, this me or this eternal soul that so many believe they have. Take the statement 'I have a soul.' This begs the question, who is the "I" that has a soul? Well then, let's reduce it to the least common denominator and say 'I am a soul.' Many may be satisfied with that but I can't help but wonder who, what or where is that soul?

Getting back to the theme of this discussion, I wish to emphasize several additional points. I contend that any individual who does not take Socrates' challenge to know oneself is leading a superficial and shallow existence.

That in and of itself is no crime and it is an individual's right of course not to wax philosophical, however, it is their loss in not experiencing the amazing power of our remarkable brains and through mindfulness practice or other forms of meditation, deepening the experience of consciousness and necessarily of life itself.

We are endowed with consciousness by nature and I contend this is the most advanced, powerful condition a living organism can attain and to borrow the cliche, it is the "universe becoming aware of itself".

We should not squander this gift! It alone is the vehicle that provides us access and allows us to operationalize the mind's inherent abilities that ultimately lead us to "know thyself". There is a popular Zen Buddhist Gatha (verse) used in meetings and services that is quite à propos to this discussion:

Let me respectfully remind you,
Life and death are of supreme importance,
Time swiftly passes by and opportunity is lost,
Each of us should strive to awaken,

AWAKEN!
TAKE HEED!
DO NOT SQUANDER YOUR LIFE!

The second key point I wish to make is that unless we undertake an introspective journey in search of ourself, the real "me," we are fated to live a shallow, materialistic existence, taking up space on the planet, functioning as a mindless consumer, a "food-bag" if you will. And this goes for the believer and atheist alike. If we do not turn our attention inward, we are unlikely to witness the somewhat chaotic flow of ideas continually competing for our attention and action.

Worse still, without the light of awareness, things will be said and actions taken without review or consideration of potential consequences and thus one acts completely upon impulse without the benefit of instinct that governs much of the rest of the animal kingdom.

The potential negative consequences of impulsive behavior can be quite unpleasant, oftentimes embarrassing and even deadly. Furthermore, another major human mental condition, emotionality, manifests as a random force when one is not aware and inwardly focused, buffeting the individual seemingly without reason, occasionally overwhelming that person with the result ranging from foolish to violent behavior.

Of course, in most cases our thoughts and emotions are not violent or potentially hazardous to oneself or others (insane) and are more likely benign or even pleasant but the fact that we (our consciousness) are either not focused or in many cases (my theory) not present at all, results in a shallow, undignified existence.

Thirdly, absent introspection or mindfulness discipline, one is perpetually caught in a web of desire, impulse and a life lacking in discipline and self-control, the result being perpetual craving and suffering. We go from one desire to the next, preoccupied with gratification so much so that when we attain a reward of some sort, we are barely able to enjoy it before the next craving arises.

We are locked in a perpetual cycle of craving and gratification or disappointment and are barely aware most of the time and consequently life passes by and we wonder where has the time gone?

Taking on the task of knowing thyself and thereby unlocking the higher powers of the mind through conscious focus inward, while not an easy thing to do and even a little frightening when one acknowledges uncertainty around personal identity, we are able to begin to understand our true nature, savor the experience of being human, participate in constructing a better "me" that is actually able to make a positive contribution to the world.

Finally, while I have attempted to present a convincing argument that we must seek to know who and what we are, in the final outcome and I hate to kill your buzz, in all likelihood you will never truly "know" who you are.

The reason being is that after many hours and even years of internal searching, meditation, contemplation or even prayer, we find the self cannot be located, and this is because there is no permanent self, no fixed identity separate from the web of reality. You, me, the experience of self, is an ever changing epiphenomenon constructed by consciousness and consisting of a stream of memories, emotions, behaviors and thoughts, drawn from various centers of the brain.

There is no little man or woman inside your brain, a substantial YOU, steering the ship! At best there is a control center, a kind of "supervisory module," a component of or result of consciousness, that when turned on (directed attention) monitors, filters, controls behaviors and provides the experience of me-ness. This is really quite remarkable and in my opinion is a gift of nature, evolution, the universe, or if you prefer, from god, to be cherished.

But take heart, all is not lost since those of us who turn inward and search for the self, search for the "me" that we feel exists via some form of introspection, mindfulness or meditation, will certainly become intimately acquainted with their total being, familiar with how their brain works, with the rising of thoughts and emotions and in time grasping intuitively, experientially their true nature, which in Zen is called enlightenment.

Once you awaken and experience of your true nature as I have attempted to describe it, you will absolutely begin to savor your existence, armed with a heightened sense of awareness of what goes on within and without, an enhanced desire and ability to improve as a person, newfound joy and compassion for and connection to all that exists.

You will find that the racing hands of your life clock begin to slow down as you learn to live in the present moment. So, don't be disappointed when, in the search for yourself you don't find what you set out to because instead of chasing a ghost, an illusion of a me that isn't there, you have found reality and are now able to truly begin living, experiencing and developing the potential abilities nature has given us and have finally taken the next step in human evolution, to a more noble, wise, enlightened state, a true homo sapiens.

Chapter 11
The Failure of Democracy

How can I possibly say this? Commie pinko, fascist, traitor! Royal ass-kisser. Well, don't kill the messenger but somebody has to say this loud enough, that democracy as a means of governance for even the smallest communities is a failure conceptually and functionally.

Many of the reasons for this assertion are based on my 73+ years as a US citizen and rudimentary knowledge of our country's history, but I suspect my objections and criticisms would apply to all so-called democratic states.

So at the risk of being accused of heresy, allow me to explain. We all know that rights of the individual, personal freedom, life, liberty and the pursuit of happiness and democratic principles are conceptually inseparable and blended in all democratic constitutions. Fine.

But as soon as you have three random people in a room debating or voting, most likely one will be unhappy with the decision of the majority and that problem is compounded exponentially with the ever-increasing size of the electorate. Just look at the political situation in the USA in 2023. We have widespread, toxic, painful culture war across a myriad of issues and ever-increasing sentiment favoring some kind of civil war. And we supposedly have the best constitution, are the "great experiment," the "greatest nation on earth".

The current minority and the former president, Trump, can't even accept the results of the last election they are so traumatized and averse to governance by the liberal majority. We have a divided, grid-locked government on our hands and no matter how you slice it, there will always be a little under half of the electorate and legislature very unhappy with the "tyranny" of the majority party.

I claim no special expertise nor special training in the science of politics, just a little common sense and over 50 years as a participant in American democracy. But no special talent is needed in order to see the multitude of problems in this country and democracy in general.

First and foremost, the rights of the individual, so precious to us all, will always be subordinate to the rights of the majority, that is unless we are all of like mind. Yeah right! We in the West have been socialized and educated to revere the rights of individual freedom and come to expect this, even demand this as part of the status quo and it just ain't happening, at least not anymore.

It is impossible in these modern times with so many diverse cultures living within the same border to function in and tolerate a monoculture where most individuals share the same beliefs and sociopolitical-economic principles. And even if they did, the differences between the sexes always present existential challenges.

Easy to see given the way men, even in so-called democracies and especially our own, have subjugated women by intimidation, force and even violence for centuries! If we read the writing on the wall, we can see that the failure of US democracy has come to a head and is ignored only at our peril.

In the not too distant past there was process, by design, consisting of debate, compromise, resolution and ultimately legislative action, whereas for the past almost 12 years there has been complete gridlock in the US Congress. Personal and political animus has replaced patriotism to the degree that the nation's physical and digital infrastructure have decayed to the point of system-wide collapses.

The highway and transportation systems are 50 years behind and dilapidated, electrical and electronic grids are inadequate and, vulnerable to hacking by hostile governments and at the same time most of our energy infrastructure systems are contributing to instead of reducing greenhouse gas emissions.

The most lethal threat to our nation and the planet as a whole, global warming, has just about reached the point of assured planet-wide biosphere devastation. We are on a fast track to a "brave new world" that may potentially spell extinction to our species and despite 98% of all climate scientists confirming the accelerating greenhouse effect and gradual but devastating damage of man-made climate heating, half of government and the population at large don't believe it and refuse to take action. Remarkable!

It is apparent to me that a primary flaw of and reason for the failure of democracy is that one of the core premises, individual freedom, is taken out of context. Given the fact that we are social animals, living in close, crowded quarters with limited resources, individual rights cannot supersede rights of society as a whole.

It is necessary that we share resources and cooperate but when we introduce all the freedoms granted in the constitution, we invariably see conflict since there is inadequate provision for balancing the rights of the individual with those of the group. We see a plethora of problems in all aspects of society ranging from racism, to sexism, religious hatred, anti LGBTQ, classism, social injustice, income inequality, poverty and on and on.

Clearly, the core principle of democracy, if it has any chance to succeed or barely function, is compromise and acceptance of the will of the majority. Without that buy-in, the government will fail and we see that happening in the early 21st century. The well-being of society (and the environment) must supersede the rights of the individual.

However, if there is to be any notion of individual freedom, there must never be legislation against so-called "victimless crimes" nor shall there be legislated morality. Finally, we need to ditch the notion of "in God We Trust" as it is unconstitutional (*shall make no law respecting an establishment of religion),* lends credibility to the religious Right and most importantly, half the population of the US is not religious!

Incompatibility of rights of the individual with the rule of the majority notwithstanding, the Constitution and Bill of Rights provide for resolution of differences but that entails a willingness to surrender some ground, to see the greater good, tolerance and perhaps most importantly, intelligence.

Clearly, these sentiments and abilities are in critically short supply. We have seen and continue to see in the majority party and this pertains mostly to the conservative, religious right when they are in power, the effort to curtail the rights of those not sharing their moral and religious perspective. They are always trying to force their skewed, Christian morality on the rest of society.

Perhaps the most egregious example of this is their continual attempt to deny women the right to choose to terminate a pregnancy. Their Christian interpretation of when a cluster of cells in a woman's body becomes a separate person is not supported by science nor is it asserted in the bible.

This, along with their tireless attempt to deny equal rights to the LGBTQ community, plus attempts to make their religious beliefs part of educational curricula in abeyance of science, represent the epitome of anti-democratic sentiment, bigotry and clear violation of the 9th Amendment 'certain rights shall not be construed to deny or disparage others retained by the people.'

Perhaps at the heart of the problem is the simple fact that despite our species' intelligence and sophisticated tech, most of us are still just one step out of the stone age, remain ignoble brutes consumed with and ruled by our baser emotions: insecurity greed, and anger. The instinct of survival has morphed into aggrandizement of the individual and such self-infatuation is at odds with the notion of government by representation, another key element of democracy.

What I am maintaining here is that due to egotism, greed and impulse, elected officials cannot be trusted to represent the best interests of their constituents. This is seen over and over and over again. First of all and perhaps the greatest detriment is the fact that federal, state and local governments have allowed wealthy private interest direct access to influence law making via lobbying, with its unlimited campaign contributions and quid pro quo.

This insidious corruption has perverted a fragile system in which virtually all elected officials are guilty. The will of the people is ignored in favor of placating the needs of wealthy individuals and big corporations.

Furthermore, the same individuals that benefit directly from this corrupt arrangement are the only ones empowered to create legislation that prevents it and what do you think they are going to do? Bite the hand that feeds? I don't think so.

Another flaw of American democracy, if not all elected governments is the fact that there are inadequate job qualifications to become eligible to run for office, if there are any prerequisites at all. Our Constitution only specifies age, origin of birth and citizenry. Not a thing about education, training or professional experience, what a pathetic joke.

To think that the highest offices in our land have no qualifications required is absurd and goes a long way to explain why the political landscape and state of the nation is in such disarray. Just think, a presidential candidate or elect does not need executive experience, prior high elected office or even a college diploma!

Members of Congress, both House and Senate, whose main responsibility is to make laws do not need a law degree, college or even a high school diploma. We get what we pay for, I guess. You think this is bad, well, read on.

Perhaps the greatest impediment to a fair and functioning democracy is the actual electorate themselves, the majority of whom are uninformed, uneducated, unintelligent. Oh, and let's not forget, apathetic, and greedy. That's right, as a group, we Americans and most other world democracies are simply too stupid. Where to start?

With regard to the electorate, most were only at best average students and many didn't even finish high school. They didn't take civics or poly-sci classes seriously and don't have a clue how democracy is supposed to work. They don't stay informed, are not objective and, for the most part are only one or two issue voters.

They are easily duped by deceptive, negative political ads. They don't care about or respect the rights of others who do not share their point of view. Many are openly hateful, racist, sexist, religious hypocrites that resist cooperation and compromise.

Of course, candidates and elected officials share the same traits and the latter are more to blame since they make the laws which are in most cases written by slick lobbyists and attorneys in such a way as to be indecipherable to the very same legislators that must vote on them, to say nothing of the impact on those of us who must abide by the "law". What ever happened to "of the people, by the people and for the people"?

Another major and tied for the worst flaw of our democracy is gerrymandering, called redistricting or apportionment the practice of which is routinely and corruptly manipulated in such a way as to allow the minority party to retain disproportionate majority rule by arbitrarily drawing borders that cram most voters of the opposite party into a few districts instead of in their neighborhoods, towns and natural geographic areas, or spread them so thinly, giving minority party control over a majority of districts that determine state and national congressional elections, most importantly the electoral college.

This aspect of our government is unethical, nondemocratic corrupt and is one of the first problems that should be corrected if we are to ever have a legitimate, functioning, fair democracy.

Let us not forget a somewhat recent contamination of democracy in the form of Citizens United v. FEC, wherein the Supreme Court asserted that corporations are people and removed reasonable campaign contribution limits, allowing a small group of wealthy donors and special interests to use dark money to influence elections.

Seriously, corporations are people? Things were bad enough with wealthy private donors installing candidates of their choice and now thanks to the Supreme Court's "Citizens United" decision corporations are now considered "persons" and big business with even more money is able to "buy" elections with their massive political campaign donations. Unconscionable.

There is no doubt in my mind that another of the worst, nondemocratic articles of our constitution is the electoral college which allows the states and not the people choose the president. To allow a candidate with three million fewer votes, e.g., Trump, to win the presidency is perhaps the ultimate antithesis of our so-called democracy and must be amended. State's rights should not supersede the rights of the majority of US citizens!

Somewhat related to the aforementioned US government rules and laws permitting tyranny by the minority is the "Catch 22" that results from the filibuster rule, wherein the Senate minority party can block a vote and even a debate if the super-majority of 60% is not achieved on any given bill.

The most disparaging component of this is that all it takes is one senator to kill a bill by filibuster, which is totally preposterous. The catch being that you can't overturn an undemocratic rule without having more than a majority, which is a contradiction of the meaning of democratic rule. What nonsense.

Allow me to cite yet another serious flaw with our American "democratic" government and one which I am sure permeates many others around the globe and that is the lack of term limits and limit on campaign contributions which go hand in hand.

The "good ole boy network" has been in effect for generations and doesn't appear likely to change since the corrupt, comfortable politicians are unlikely to give up their power and influence, so we are stuck with incapable officials controlled by the 1% and big corporations.

Consequently, real debate and action on the needs of the people never see the light of day. Oh, and irony of ironies, guess who the only ones that can fix this problem are? That's right, the same ones who get rich and abuse power as a result of no term limits, the US Congress! Oh, and let's not forget they even approve their own raises and lavish fringe benefits, whatever happened to the merit system?

Perhaps the last major flaw of our democracy worth mentioning in this discussion is the two-party system. I know, tweedle dee or tweedle dum. First and foremost it does not come close to representing the national electorate culturally or politically since there are numerous other parties that get votes including Libertarian, Green and Constitutional parties.

And there are others of lesser note but with sizable followings including the Socialist, Communist, Tea Party and New Democrats. Probably the largest political third faction that is not an official party yet represents millions of voters and several Congress members is the Independents.

Our two party, winner-take all system has always been rancorous and now has become totally grid-locked and virtually ineffectual and if we are to survive as a nation must be replaced. Most other so-called democracies have a much better idea that uses a multi-party system with its proportional representation, often in the form of a parliament wherein different parties frequently form coalitions in order to achieve a majority and thus seat a government.

In this way, minority parties participate and can obtain a voice in government, how novel. We are just too big and too diverse politically, ideologically, culturally, morally, academically and religiously for a "one size fits all" system where millions never have candidates with shared ideals, thus virtually no representation, and as a result are left to vote for the "lesser of two evils" and never fully achieve representation in the system.

As a result, many millions of citizens simply drop out of the political process and this is not how a democracy should function.

Chapter 12
The Myth of Intelligence

Webster defines intelligence as 1) 'the ability to learn, understand or deal with new or trying situations, "REASON" and 2) 'the ability to apply knowledge to manipulate one's environment or to think abstractly as measured by objective criteria (such as tests).'

Allow me to offer another take on the definition by the famous astrophysicist Neil deGrasse Tyson, 'Intelligence is just the right thing to have (in order) to render yourself extinct.' Is he being sarcastic, facetious or purely cynical?

Actually, none of the above and sadly, he is just being realistic. His statement issues to all who read or hear it a dire warning and captures the essence of my concern in writing this chapter. In fact, his concern is a reiteration of the sentiments of his idol and mentor (and one of mine as well) Carl Sagan, who, over 40 years ago issued multiple warnings to mankind regarding our penchant for environmental devastation as well as flirtation with nuclear mutual self-destruction.

The concept of intelligence is complex and clearly we can see that our species has over millions of years demonstrated the ability to learn, deal with trying situations and manipulate environments in order to survive. We have evolved and advanced the species "homo sapiens" to the big-brained, highly "intelligent" creature we find ourselves today. But something is wrong with that picture.

We certainly exhibit several of the abilities that qualify us as intelligent i.e., learns, thinks, deals with, applies and manipulates. But perhaps the two most important skills in Webster's definition of intelligence, Understands and Reasons, are not so easily claimed by us. Furthermore, I contend that another critical ability must be considered a constituent of intelligence and that is 'applies knowledge and manipulates environment with positive intent and regards and takes responsibility for consequences.'

More on this later but back to understanding and reason. Do we really possess and display those qualities? Sometimes? All the time? Individually? As a group?

According to Webster, Reason is 'the power of the mind to think, understand, and form judgments by a process of logic.' Webster defines Understanding as "comprehension" and that is still not clear enough so I'll list some additional synonyms to help elucidate understanding: 'apprehend, grasp, see, take in, perceive, discern, make out, puzzle out, recognize, keep up with, master, get to know, follow, fathom, get to the bottom of, penetrate, divine, interpret, unravel, decipher, see the light about, envisage.'

Now we're getting somewhere. Intelligence is an incredibly complex and demanding mistress and we are not measuring up!

So, I have entitled this chapter "the myth of intelligence," why so skeptical? Primarily because when we look at the collective accomplishments of our species, with our impressive brains, looking at the state of the environment and society today, we see overwhelming destruction, suffering and chaos.

WE have not acted intelligently and despite residing on the brink of global climate catastrophe, we continue to argue and waste time. We continue to breed out of control, vastly over-populating the Earth and with that, continue to mindlessly consume and waste precious resources. We are messy slobs and deposit our trash and waste everywhere without regard to the point that the oceans are polluted and the land littered and contaminated.

Since the dawn of history and I am sure before that we have slaughtered our own kind and continue to do so but not in quantities sufficient to keep our numbers in check. Nature provides predation, disease, harsh weather and food scarcity for that purpose but we have been clever enough to overcome nature in that one respect. Haha, I guess the laugh is on us.

See, in Webster's definition of intelligence are "Reason and Understanding" and I would add another, Beneficence and clearly the net result of human activity to date is severely lacking in those three critical qualities.

We are truly naïve and arrogant when we boast of our intelligence as a species. Surely there have been numerous discoveries, inventions and works of art down through the ages but these are individual accomplishments.

I repeat, individual accomplishments that the rest of us cannot take credit for. The fact is, very few positive, if any, beneficial, environmental accomplishments can be attributed to societies or civilizations. Clearly, we haven't yet arrived as an "intelligent species" since our ability to reason and understand and learn from our mistakes as a species has not manifested.

We are one of nature's works in progress, an evolutionary experiment that is about to fail big-time if we don't get our shit together in a hurry. And as a reasonable, sentient, compassionate human, a citizen of Earth in his last quartile of life, I am, quite frankly, pretty pissed!

There is so much beauty, joy and knowledge to celebrate in this life and we do have great brains and so much potential to evolve further, yet at the same time have so much hatred, suffering and destruction. As a species, I believe we are facing our final test and things are looking bleak.

Isn't it a little ironic when you think about it, we evolved to be social creatures and the ability to work together in groups enabled us not only to survive, but to thrive and evolve further and develop amazing intellectual talents. My god, some of our brightest minds have unraveled the mysteries of the universe and taken us back to the beginning of time!

My point is this, humanity is playing a dangerous, deadly, extinction-level game with very little time to turn things around so as things stand right now we do not qualify as an intelligent species. We have our wake-up call, now all we need is an epiphany. We need once and for all to accelerate the dawning of a new sub-species, I will call "Enlightened Man," one that leaves its violent survival instincts behind and truly begins to manifest the wonderful potential nature has endowed us with!

Chapter 13
The Truth About Capitalism

There should be little argument that capitalism promotes hard work, initiative, creativity, investment and that it rewards many of its successful practitioners. It also has proven to be an economic boon in nations who embrace it and surprisingly that includes communist countries as well, as antithetical as that may seem. If only Adam Smith had lived to see the evolution of the economic system he developed, he would be blown away.

Capitalistic principles are primarily responsible for the industrial revolution and ushering the age of modern western civilization with all its conveniences, luxuries, technology and let us not forget armageddon capable war machines! It also systematized for the already prosperous merchant class and "nobility" the ultimate tool for the creation of vast wealth, "legitimization of unlimited, unquestioned greed"!

That's right, greed is good and no justification is needed, in capitalism the means justify the ends and the ends are profit. Sadly, the system is predicated on one of the baser, ignoble and dominant of human emotions rather than love and compassion. The great eastern prophet, Buddha, taught that greed (endless craving) is one of the primary causes of human suffering and he nailed it, don't you agree?

There, I've said it, capitalism is potentially, inherently evil, or perhaps I should say it promotes, glorifies and legitimizes the human traits we actually need less rather than more of. Can anyone in good conscience say we need more greed in the world? Isn't there enough without making it the cornerstone of over two-thirds of the world's economies? And do we really need more competition, the second key aspect of capitalism?

At over 7.5 billion, the world is vastly overcrowded and what is really needed is cooperation. And finally, do we need a global system of non-sustainable mass production of consumer goods?

Look where these economic forces have gotten us. Capitalism is driven by profit and profit is created by sales growth and that is driven by an ever-increasing consumer base and the process doesn't take long, just a few generations and voila!

We have a bloated, polluting, manufacturing mania on our hands with a relative handful of uber rich, mega billionaires taking us down a road to ruin while they make plans to go live on Mars! What a freaking mess we have here, and what is the point? I am waiting for somebody to please tell me there is a cultural or evolutionary benefit or justification to all the global, industrial oligarchs have wrought! I am not holding my breath.

You know what really galls and astonishes me at the same time? Everywhere you look, people don't seem to have a clue as to the disorganized chaos we are living in. Stores are filled with a lot of useless, plastic junk, shoppers are loading up on it and always on the lookout for the latest fad and the hottest sale. Business and industry keep finding clever ways to mass produce and distribute said junk and they, especially PRC, are now eyeing ways to infect the 3rd world along with the rest of modern society.

Heaven forbid, agrarian and hunter-gatherer tribal societies be left alone and allowed to live in harmony with nature, on the land, without modern conveniences and religions. Just leave them alone and while we're at it, leave the Amazon Rain Forest alone, or else! I challenge anybody to justify and argue successfully for a truly positive cultural, societal end game of the high-tech, consumer-based global economy we have been sucked into.

I don't see the betterment of society or the advancement of civilization, but rather mostly billions of clueless consumers, ubiquitous excessive consumption and mountains of trash and nasty seepage everywhere. Oh yes and lest I forget one positive result, job creation, but most importantly to the downside, a growing, global, mostly selfish billionaire's club.

I feel like I am "beating a dead dog" here and I guess that is not entirely unintentional. Perhaps it would be better to stand on a corner beating a drum and crying "the end is near," because it is, unless we take stock and redirect economies to sustainable, more humanistic activities.

I am at a loss as to what can be done since the problems facing humanity are so obvious and closely tied to the pandemic of global capitalism, which is even employed by fascist and so-called communist states, with the subsequent, seemingly inevitable results being over-population and environmental devastation.

Compounding this massive problem, the masses are completely caught up in their daily drama and world leaders are unwilling or incapable of acting and the ones who hold the real power, the 1%, are too greedy and shortsighted to see that the consumerist house of cards they have built is beginning to collapse and there is no stopping it. Where are the "philosopher kings" when you need them? Certainly not in the person of a Bezos, Musk or Zuckerberg!

Over several hundred years capitalism has gone from a means of supplying the masses with essential goods and services to a resource gobbling, greenhouse gas belching, environment trashing, Planet Destroyer! One can't argue how successful it has been as a means of production and "wealth creation". And it has raised the global standard of living to one in which billions of us lack for nothing with regard to life's essentials and that in itself is not so bad.

However, the mass production of home goods and groceries has stimulated demand for workers and the resultant high standard of living has led to a global population explosion, exponential growth in demand for products and subsequently exhaustion of natural resources along with toxic pollution of much of the natural environment.

The genie, "profit," has been let out of the bottle and it is too late to put him back in, as if that were even possible. Profit is just another sugar coated term for "greed" and there seems to be no limit to it. At this late in the game, the global economic engine is a runaway train and despite the efforts of some to introduce sustainability and moderation it may be too late to turn things around.

Chapter 14
The Failure to Teach Life Skills

As a baby boomer, I grew up with the educational system, both public and private, still locked in to the 100+ year old 3 Rs, "readin, ritin, and rithmetic" philosophy, with maybe a dash of science, civics, history, art and music thrown in. All well and good and due to the dedication, charisma and creativity of many of my teachers, I learned a good bit about the world around me but went on to the school of hard knocks, called real life, somewhat ill-prepared.

Back in the day and I mean all the way back to the beginning of formal educational systems for the masses, kids were taught a trade, taken in as apprentices, (girls were overlooked) or maybe even went to a school where basic writing, math and science were taught in preparation for a career in which actual job skills could then be refined in the workplace.

Throughout human history, and this is at best a casual observation, I see little evidence, at least in Western societies, of life skills being taught. Think I'm wrong? There's a hot professional field that has grown up over the last 20 or so years called Certified Life Coach and their task is to help us adults get our shit together. Shouldn't that curriculum be a component in the educational system?

I have little doubt that most educators, parents and even the church would claim teaching life skills is the purview of the home but judging from the chaotic state of society in the US and most of the world it is obvious that is not being done. You may know, as I have, several friends from your school years who always knew what they wanted to be (fireman, astronaut) or chose a career path, got a degree, got a job in that field and lived happily ever after. Well, it is my contention those individuals are in a small minority. You may have also known a couple kids, back then boy and girl, who became high school sweethearts, got married right after graduation, boy got job, girl started housekeeping and raising babies and good chance probably struggled and finally divorced after 10 years.

Today's problems in learning how to live in the world are much more complex and considerably more daunting than they were back in the leave it to beaver era. The modern world is much more complex and challenging with the myriad choices and costs of educational and career training enough to leave your head spinning. Too much, in my opinion, for an 18-year-old to make informed choices on what to do for the rest of their life.

And if the technical complexity and competition in the modern world weren't enough, we now have an emergent, deepening extremely divisive culture war in the US and much of the world, as well as ongoing, violent religious and racial strife as well as genocide.

Add to this the lethal global economic rivalry of capitalism vs socialism and the toxic political rivalry of war-mongering communist vs democratic states and we have some major, on-going, potentially catastrophic local and global problems for the human race and I believe the widespread failure to teach our children how to live in this crazy world is a large part of the problem.

As you may have guessed by now, the main point of this book is to bring attention to problems facing humanity and Mother Earth that, in the opinion of a person in the autumn of his life, have not been addressed adequately or in some cases even acknowledged and the shit is hitting the fan. The older I get, the more frustrated, outraged and spurred to act I get, as should we all.

Given our capabilities, there is no excuse for not fixing the mess we have made and we need to start yesterday and make haste. The doomsday clock is counting down and is dangerously close to midnight.

To fix the world's problems we need to fix society and to fix society entails fixing individuals and I contend our only hope of doing that effectively is to nurture and educate people while they are still malleable, the period spanning childhood through young adulthood, and the best means for that is the educational system.

It ain't happening in the home, where in many cases they are just picking up the same bad habits of their parents, either through modeling or active instruction, where more often than not home lessons will be of little benefit and can in fact be harmful since prejudices and misinformation are passed on.

No offense but most parents are not remotely qualified, nor do they have the time to teach their children and one can only hope that they instill a sense of self-worth, morality, feeling loved, curiosity and personal responsibility. The early infancy and pre-K years are the most important in the formation of a well-adjusted, emotionally intact humans prepared to enter society and unfortunately, in my opinion, most parents are ill-prepared, and/or simply too busy with work to perform this task.

Judging from the innumerable ills of society, I think that is all the proof one should need. But getting back to the discussion of the shortcomings of the educational system, given the fact that so many children enter school with some emotional issues or poor socialization skills, the hope for not only teaching but also bolstering self-esteem and assuaging emotional trauma become the de-facto responsibility of the schools and in particular, dependent on the skills of the teachers.

Schools must improve the education process and produce healthy, smart, well-adjusted youth or WE are screwed. Here are some suggestions:

Daycare, Pre-K and K

- Emphasis on socialization, cooperative play and games.
- Focus on self-esteem evaluation and development, ego formation.
- Teachers must have training in child psychology, social psychology.

- Emphasis on appropriate exercise and manual skill development.
- Intro to fine arts, music, language, math, science, nature, ecology.
- Assess and teach healthy eating.

1st–6th Grades

- Racial and religious diversity training.
- Continuing work on socialization skills and self-esteem.
- Environmentalism.
- Aptitude testing and tailored instruction.
- Cooperative learning.
- Compassion.
- The Family, work, careers and money.
- Friendly competition.

7th–12th Grades

- The human family.
- Protecting Earth.
- Bullying mitigation.
- Sexual relations.
- Ethnocentrism.
- Critical thinking.
- Self-Reliance.
- Mindfulness.
- Effective communicating; written and verbal.

- Economics, business and managing money.
- Improving government.
- Pragmatic plans for your future.

Post-Secondary

- Why you are here?
- How to pay for your education?
- Where the jobs are/will be?
- Personal Finances.
- Logic, statistics, critical thinking.
- Realities of marriage and having children.
- Philosophy, Reality, the meaning of life.
- Sustainable lifestyles.
- Political harmony.
- Mandatory psych evaluation and counseling as needed.
- Comprehensive job hunting and placement.

Obviously education and raising our children is one of the most difficult and challenging things we do and the educational system(s) can for a large part be held responsible for quality of young adults it turns out and ultimately for the state of society.

Of course, the impact of family and home life is of primary importance when it comes to the formation of physically and emotionally intact children and there are myriad problems that children bring from home when they enter the educational system.

That is why physical and emotional health of children's needs to be a top priority for schools and there is no "one size fits all" if we truly intend to teach our kids. As much as possible, there needs to be an assessment of each child's home life and the impact it has in his/her development along with an effort made to correct or enhance said home environment.

In many cases, the kids will be well adjusted, reasonably healthy, fertile ground for learning but many are not and subsequently efforts to teach them will fall far short.

The schools represent the last opportunity to facilitate nurturing physical and emotional well-being and that is why I say from day care on up, teachers and curricula must perform a complete intellectual and psychological wellness assessment on each child and fine-tune individual programs that bring to bear all the resources of the community including nutritional, health, socialization and parental involvement.

A final thought pertaining to this discussion. One would think that it shouldn't be the case that socialization and learning life skills are not happening in the home. In fact, it seems likely that both parties in the equation are assuming that this task will be accomplished by the other and we know that is simply not happening. Or they are simply not thinking about it at all!

The focus of this chapter has been to enable and place a majority of the responsibility of teaching life skills on the schools. However, let us not forget the critical need for children to acquire and develop emotionally and socially during the early years and in most cases this process must occur in the home.

Therefore, let me suggest the following. We all know that most of life's critical privileges and professions require some kind of training and/or licensure, think driving, flying, doctor, lawyer and gun owner. Even the most personal of all, marriage, also requires a license and many churches even mandate marriage counseling.

Well, since bearing and raising children is certainly one of the most important and challenging tasks we all take on, in light of the failure of the current scenario of child rearing (just look at the predicament of humanity) it is time to consider requiring parenting instruction, financial means and emotional maturity all a prerequisite to obtaining a permit to have a child.

Sound a little like big brother? Maybe but it is a completely logical, rational notion and in fact would synch up well with my recommendation to formalize socialization and life skills instruction in the educational system.

Given the plight of humanity and the myriad problems on our planet, all of our own making, one must question the limits of personal freedom and the "right" to bear as many children as we choose regardless of parental and educational system's ability to adequately raise them and the Earth's resources to sustain the human family. The success of our species depends on our ability to raise intelligent well-adjusted children and heretofore our track record has not been good enough.

Chapter 15
The Big Scary
Bogeyman SOCIALISM!

I would like to turn my attention to perhaps one of the biggest, loudest, dumbest, right-wing, political dog whistles of our time, "Socialist"! If you can believe it, quite possibly even scarier than "taking our guns" and "baby killers".

The inescapable irony with regard to the extreme aversion to socialism is the fact that those who are most opposed to it in principle and practice, conservative leaning poor and working class, are the ones who actually benefit most from its implementation.

By definition, socialism is a political/economic system wherein the people (government) collectively own the means of production, distribution and revenue, all of which in principle are allocated equally. In a socialist country, the people rely on government to provide food, medicine, healthcare, education, jobs, transportation and most of the goods and services necessary for survival.

Now I consider myself a progressive, left-leaning liberal but even I don't advocate or approve of government ownership and control of all property and enterprise. And listen carefully right-wingers, hardly anybody in the US does!

This irrational fear of socialism/communism started in the 1950s with the rise of McCarthyism and the Domino Theory which eventually led to the US "manufacturing" one of the most brutal, immoral, unjust, disastrous military debacles in our history, the Vietnam War. The 1960s right-wing, military-industrial complex controlled propaganda machine, manufactured enough fear asserting that like a domino, if Vietnam fell to communism, there would be no stopping the spread and it would simply be a matter of time before the US and the free world would be overtaken!

As history now informs us, this was a deception and a huge false alarm and the minds of much of our government and society at the time were manipulated by far-right, paranoid, power brokers.

Interestingly, Vietnam seems to have forgiven us though we have never apologized to them for the death and devastation we inflicted nor have we made reparations. Vietnam remains a communist country in name but acts more like a capitalist state and is a major trading partner of ours.

Oh, and hard as it is to believe, communism did not take over SE Asia! Yet this anti-socialist, irrational fear permeates our politics and culture to this day. One has to wonder, why haven't they taken us over yet?

This is just another example of ignorant, under-educated, easily influenced, right-wing electorate being routinely distracted and manipulated by fear mongering demigods such as Trump. And before him the Bushes, Reagan and Nixon. To cite the last good, rational, true patriotic Republican President one has to go way back to Eisenhower and by the way, he was a socialist, meaning an advocate of big government as evidenced by the federal Interstate Highway System he built. Oh my.

So one thing I really don't get about the far-right's fear and loathing of socialism is the fact that we have so many government programs that are critical to the health and welfare of our citizens and many of the loudest critics happily cash their checks every month and I am referring to social security.

Millions depend on it in their retirement, I know I do and should we abolish it? What is so wrong about the government helping to take care of its citizens, especially those in need? And who is being hurt by wealth redistribution when there is so much in this country?

And the same can be said about Medicare and Medicaid. They are literally life savers and provide access to healthcare that otherwise would be financially out of reach for many, subsequently saving lives and preventing financial ruin. I am a boomer and it blows my mind that so many of my generation, in fact over 50%, fear the socialist boogeyman and support far right, fascist leaning candidates and at the same time have no qualms about taking social security and Medicare. Ignorant hypocrites!

When you look closely, all of us, even the 1% are affected by and benefit from government funded (socialist) programs and in fact over half of federal, state and local government tax revenues are allocated to programs benefiting we the people including:

- Public Schools
- Public Parks
- Libraries
- Food stamps
- College grants
- Law enforcement grants
- National Parks
- HUD/Housing Assistance
- Head start
- Energy Assistance
- Coast Guard
- Internet
- FTC
- FDIC
- SEC
- And on and on!

One last point, if I may. All of this socialism hysteria being whipped up by the neocon, MAGA (Make America Great Again) politicians is sadly duping so many not so politically savvy voters into actually voting against their self-interest. Perhaps the best, most glaring example is the massive Trump era trillion-dollar tax cut that mainly benefited the 1% and big corporations for which "we" the 99% will be paying for, for generations.

All the anti-socialist, fascists who elected that bunch, must only believe in social programs for the rich, not people who actually work for, deserve and need them and could do something constructive with the money.

Back to my last point. All the socialist witch hunting, paranoid accusations by right wing politicos and manufactured false stereotypes over generations and I ask you, where is the commie/socialist take over? Has it happened yet? Did we miss it?

Duh, I guess it hasn't happened nor will it ever and that is because nobody, especially the libs, dems, left or whatever don't want it and aren't in any way pursuing a socialist takeover. Just fairness and equal opportunity for all and the uber-rich just paying their fair share.

Remember, we have a virtually bullet-proof Constitution that requires a 2/3 majority in Congress and 2/3 of the states for just one amendment. It is inconceivable that the entire document ever be rewritten to reflect a transition to socialist principles, that is unless most of the country actually wanted it and then that would be OK wouldn't it?

Chapter 16
The 1% Are Responsible for Global Warming

Not only are the top 1% wealth and income brackets responsible for global warming but they are also to blame for most of the other socio-economic problems facing humanity. WHAT?

In a nutshell, the rich have promulgated, funded and built the industrial revolution and their insatiable greed has imposed a wasteful, energy guzzling, carbon emitting, frivolous, consumer economy on the planet and voila, 200 years later we have dangerously over-heated (and polluted) Earth. We all, including scientists and engineers, have been willing participants, enablers to a certain extent in this high-risk carbon-based, energy consumption fiasco! We have happily driven our cars and cranked up the AC for over a century and now things are getting desperate.

The UN has been grappling with the problem since the late 1980s and despite the repeated warnings of climate scientists, this "Inconvenient Truth" (thanks Al Gore) has become a more than inconvenient crisis on its way to a disaster. It should be quite clear by now that world governments are unwilling and unable to act and they have had plenty of time.

So it leaves just one, final option. The 1% are directly responsible for making the mess so they need to clean it up and fast! Especially if they want to remain uber-rich and retain the actual power and control over our destiny. Massive investments are needed immediately in every available technology and every sector toward the goal of Net Zero Global Carbon emissions.

The super rich are not saddled with bureaucracy and to the same degree so are many of the big corporations so they too must act and I mean fast.

Now just because I have laid out the case for whom is primarily responsible for climate change and impending global disaster and whom is able and responsible for mitigating it, that doesn't get the rest of us 99 percenters off the hook.

We are all, and I am referring to modern, technological, consumer, manufacturing societies, culpable to a significant degree as we have been participants, enablers if you will, in that we provided a market for all the carbon sourced junk the industrial barons have determined we need as well as gladly bred enough workers to support the effort.

I am deliberately excluding primitive, tribal cultures and to some extent 3rd world countries as they don't have a clue and simply follow their instinct to survive. Additionally, despite the fact that the 1%, through their manufacturing, have produced and sold us the climate altering products over generations, that doesn't mean wasteful consumerism must remain the case.

We, the masses, the buyers of products must immediately begin to express our sentiments in opposition to high carbon emitting goods and services in the marketplace by squelching our desire for big SUV's, pickups and riding lawn mowers. And we must make every effort to demand and buy climate friendly hybrids and EVs.

Whether or not you agree with my contention that the rich are responsible for the current mounting climate crisis, my insistence that they are on the hook for fixing things is a no brainer.

The most obvious reason why they should fix the climate, i.e., flood the marketplace with carbon neutral products and/or simply purchase and implement green energy systems with their own funds is this: only the rich have the liquidity and as a group, the trillions of dollars that are required to make the global scale greenhouse gas reduction investments.

The uber-rich oligarchs and the mega corporations like Apple, Google, Amazon, Tesla and Microsoft are flush with trillions of spare cash and the immediate thing for them and all cash heavy global corporations is to fast track their own carbon footprints to net-zero. Massive investments in carbon neutral renewables will not only spur further investments across the economy but also provide new job growth, energy savings which improve the bottom line and modernization of the electrical grid.

Anyway, what is the alternative? In 30 years to watch society crumble and along with that, the global economy and thus the personal and corporate trillions melt away? Clearly, this is the only option and a necessary first step, otherwise humanity is doomed!

Now just because I have laid out the argument that the super-rich are primarily responsible for the climate crisis and instrumental in what should be an urgent effort to slow and hopefully halt global warming, it doesn't absolve the rest of us, including the ordinary rich (6 and 7 figure earners) and all large cap, mid-cap and even "small businesses," from taking aggressive action to dramatically reduce their carbon footprints.

Far and away, the best things to do in terms of quick impact that carry little to NO financial investment are energy conservation initiatives. Business, government and private sector all need to be turning lights off, turning AC higher, heat lower, driving less, planning trips, walking and biking more, purchasing Energy Star appliances and many more.

The next best thing to do is make energy efficiency improvements on existing buildings such as adding adequate insulation, caulking, weatherstripping, thermopane windows and Energy Star heating and cooling. All of these things have a payback and a big impact on the carbon footprint. For those that can afford to, there are home solar electric systems, electric vehicles, hybrids, wind and geothermal heat.

Needless to say the uber-rich, mega corporations and even the one percenters need to be fast-tracking investments in carbon neutral technology for home and business, transportation and most importantly the electrical grid and physical plant infrastructure. All the above-mentioned measures apply, the main difference being scale and investment in innovative carbon neutral technologies.

Alongside striving for personal and corporate net-zero, the rich **must** invest their massive wealth in local, national and global climate change mitigation projects. I am sure given their abilities to manage and acquire wealth they will find a way to secure tax credits, charitable deductions and almost certainly generate revenue and profit.

Having said that, the rest of us, including governments, are not exempt and the entire human population must be doing everything we possibly can as soon as possible or we risk irreversible climate catastrophe and quite possibly extinction of our species! Please believe this could come as soon as the dawning of the next century.

What have we got to lose by becoming conservationists, saving energy, cleaning up pollution, advancing tech in a good way and most importantly investing in our grandchildren's future?

It is so crazy that I and many of my fellow Boomers have been practicing environmentalism since reading Rachel Carson's "Silent Spring" and conserving energy since the OPEC oil embargo of the mid 70s, and here we are 50 some years later, facing a global climate crisis and the masses don't seem to have a clue and/or don't give a shit. It bogles the mind.

The science of climate change is irrefutable, well documented and has been in the public eye since the 90s. We all owe Al Gore a huge debt of gratitude for his "An Inconvenient Truth" as that documentary finally pushed the problem into the public forum once and for all and in my opinion started the final countdown to climate change disaster.

The early climate change "deniers" in Congress and the White House were instrumental in thwarting US government activities and they continue their stubborn, ignorant, anti-science efforts to obstruct at every turn and ultimately share the blame for the disaster that is immanent. Their votes against mitigation legislation make it crystal clear that they are bought and paid for by energy producers, big oil and big coal, who bear a disproportionate responsibility for the emergent climate crisis and global chaos that is immanent.

The present, all-consuming, seemingly irreconcilable culture war notwithstanding, there is one other major weapon in the war on climate disaster that has been vastly underutilized, if not ignored and it is *public information and education* on a global level.

As I stated earlier, besides massive investment in carbon neutral infrastructure by the 1% (I imagine the 5% too), given the widespread ignorance and lack of climate change mitigation activities in the majority of societies around the world, along with the critical need for every person on Earth to engage in conservation and green energy usage, the broadest possible public relations information campaign is critical.

All the key "influencers," from academia, to big business, to social media, MSM, to government and even religious organizations must participate by crafting effective messaging to all levels of their constituencies, and that includes presenting clear, incontrovertible proof of humanity caused global warming along with a recurring promotions of all practical measures individuals and businesses can take as well as access to a variety of resources. And this must be ramped up ASAP!

In the final analysis, while WE will be affected in various ways on varying timetables, it is just a matter of time before the climate disaster affects one and all. We can see the signs already in drought and flood induced crop failures prompting an exodus of "climate refugees," unprecedented forest fires, sea level rise and tidal flooding, noticeable, uncomfortable temperature increases even in the far norther latitudes, urban flooding, unseasonable storms, tornados and so much more.

It boggles the mind that more people don't see what is happening and are moved to take action, I guess that speaks to the ignorance, greed and lack of mental clarity that affects so much of humanity. Despite all the barriers and the rapid, advanced state of climate degradation, humanity must find a way to pull together as one mind and do everything within our power to slow, halt and hopefully reverse global warming!

Chapter 17
US Constitution
Woefully Obsolete!

What an outrageous claim! Unpatriotic! Ungrateful! Well, not really. Think about it. The US Constitution (USC) was written and passed by delegates of the Philadelphia Convention in 1787, that's 236 years ago.

With respect to understanding modern principles of democratic governance, much has changed since. With respect to an understanding of principles of civil and gender rights, we are finally, fully emancipated, at least morally and intellectually. Noblesse Oblige, which was the status quo then, is no longer (should no longer be) the status quo.

Furthermore, the knowledge base and educational level, along with the scientific understanding of the world we live in has advanced immeasurably. Don't get me wrong, I have considerable admiration for what the Founding Fathers (FF) accomplished and this done under great duress, and I am extremely grateful for having been born in the USA and the rights and opportunities afforded me, but the USC and the Bill of Rights (BOR) are flawed, obsolete and woefully limited in scope.

Furthermore, the FF were wealthy noblemen, the majority being slave owners, all members of just one faith, christianity, and to the man blatantly sexist! Given these biases and perhaps a few other lesser quirks and flaws, the credibility and applicability of the documents, especially the USC and the BOR must be called into question.

Before commenting on the obsolete and non-libertarian biases and flaws of the USC and BOR, I wish to raise what is to me an obvious point of contention and that is its language. We must ask, is the English language changing?

The answer is **yes**, and so is every other human language. Language is always changing, evolving, and adapting to the needs of its users and I contend that the language of the time, the King's English, is obtuse, primitive and in many ways unintelligible to us 21st Century descendants and the language of the FF has been and continues to be either misunderstood, subject to continual re-interpretation and at times comes across as moderate gibberish, unless one is a linguist with a law degree.

For example, Olde English, like other old Germanic languages, it is very different from Modern English, and largely incomprehensible for Modern English speakers without study.

Within Olde English grammar, nouns, adjectives, pronouns and verbs have many inflectional endings and forms, and word order is much freer. Consequently, this is the case for what is considered the language of the FF, "Modern English" while American English or US English is the divergent dialect of the English language now spoken in the United States of America. It is different even in some ways from other types of Modern English, such as British English.

So what this boils down to is that accurate understanding of the language and much of the meaning and original intent of the USC and BOR are forever lost to time and subsequently open to widely varying interpretation by the Supreme Court, Congress, President and citizens and consequently demands a complete review and updating if not a complete rewrite consistent with a contemporary, fair, unambiguous interpretation of modern democratic principles.

If you think about it, you will realize that the FF would want it reviewed, corrected and updated and in fact did precisely that with the first Constitutional Convention and the first 12 Amendments, the BOR, just three years later!

Another major, major problem with the USC is the question of the credibility of the framers. I know, how outrageous. But they are just men, not gods and their "BOOK" is not handed down from God. As such, I see that there are two major issues pertaining to credibility that must not, cannot be ignored and I am talking about their morality and humanity. Specifically, and this is the first one, they not only condoned but most of them actually owned slaves and codified it in the USC!

I don't care what era we are talking about, slavery is a crime against humanity, the most cruel, brutal, violent, immoral, unimaginable act that one human being can commit against another! And anyone who condones it forfeits their credibility and membership in the family of man! Did Christ own slaves? Would he have?

It is hard to imagine why slavery is not forbidden in the Ten Commandments. Perhaps an update is needed there too, God!

The second major question of the FF's credibility is the fact that women were treated as chattel, denied the right to vote and in fact were not even considered citizens!

Here again, regardless of the historical timeframe, it is unconscionable to regard women as property, accorded fewer rights than men, despite the claim that all "men" are created equal. Did god intend women to be less than men simply because they were created from Adam's rib?

Here, we see the origination of the myth of male superiority in the Old Testament and the perpetuation of it in the USC. When examining the grand design for forming a truly free, democratic society and a more perfect union, the chauvinism and racism of the FF is undeniable and it usurps the value of the documents and at the same time compels us to undertake a comprehensive review and rewrite.

Despite the aforementioned criticisms, we cannot discount the entire effort, with all the good legislation and codification that was accomplished and make no mistake, much of the USC and BOR were certainly ahead of their time and much of it is more or less relevant 235 years later.

Furthermore, despite the flaws, confusion, widely disparate interpretation, the outright misinterpretation and subsequent political disharmony and more recently infectious culture war, I am grateful to have been born in the USA with the rights and opportunities that have been afforded us, particularly being able to challenge our founding principles, documents and the mindset of the framers themselves.

At the same time, I remain haunted by the sins of slavery and sexism that persisted for so long. Going forward, please indulge my attempt to clarify some of the sections and amendments that are, in my opinion, either antiquated, wrongly interpreted or outright false.

The Preamble

The opening line 'We the People,' is much too broad and based on the subsequent writings, should have been 'We the white, Christian, males.' Furthermore, 'secure the blessings of liberty' was also not true in that it was intended only for white men, to the exclusion of Black Slaves, native Americans and all women.

Article.1.
Section.2.

Members of the House of Representatives 'shall be chosen every second year.' This is a commonly acknowledged bad idea, at least in modern times in that the congresspersons are always in a state of campaigning instead of focusing on the people's business.

- The term "Electors" is first used here and not defined as far as I can tell and this is a big problem.
- The term "Citizen" is used and not defined. Another big problem.

- 'The number of Representatives shall not exceed one for every thirty thousand.' While the number is now limited to 435, the House membership is far too large and unwieldy and consideration should be given to reducing it.
- Paragraph 3. I believe the phrase 'Bound to Service' is a euphemism for the legitimization of slavery!

Section.3.

'The Senate of the United States shall be composed of two Senators from each state.' This is inherently undemocratic in that it affords too little power to heavily populated states and too much to sparsely populated ones. Revise to a max of 300 Senators, with a minimum of two for each state up to five million population, then one more senator for each additional five million population, or some similar proportional formula.

Section.8.

'The Congress shall: provide for calling forth the militia—' Eliminate this obsolete dangerous function as we have already seen it inspire violent aggression in the minds of far-right leaning, fringe groups and most importantly there is no longer a need for militia with the formation of the National Guard and Reserves.

Article.2.
Pertains to the Office of the President
Section.1.

'He shall hold his office during the term of four years'—. Change to he "or SHE" shall—for a single term of SIX years. The highest office in the land should functionally match the 6-year term of Senators in order to focus on the business of the people and not getting reelected.

'Each state shall appoint…a number of electors'—This clause, created the electoral college, is undemocratic, corruptible, does not represent the will of the people and should be eliminated!

Section.4.

Pertains to Impeachment. Needs to be much more clearly defined as to what constitutes impeachable offenses and while the House may bring charges and impeach, actual conviction or acquittal must not be a political process, i.e., by the Senate but rather by the courts, probably the Supreme Court.

Article.3.

'The judicial power—shall be vested in one Supreme Court.'

Selection of the Supreme Court Justices should not be a partisan process but rather they should be elected by the people in national elections, must be non-partisan, have prior experience of at least 10 years at District Court level and should be term limited at 20 years. Amendments to the Constitution of the United States of America (Bill of Rights).

Amendment 1.

'Congress shall make no law respecting the establishment of religion.'

Given this very important amendment, all religious references to God or a deity should be removed from documents, oaths, government and state mottos, emblems etc., meaning no use of the phrase "in God we trust" as this is antithetical.

'—make no law abridging the freedom of speech—'

Clearly, there are forms of speech that should not be unrestricted and these pertain to hatred, bigotry, misogyny, racism and religious persecution. This is perhaps one of the most troubling issues when it comes to individual freedom and legitimizes slander. Where to draw the line is a very complicated matter, given how inflammatory and destructive hate speech can be.

Amendment 2

'A well-regulated militia being necessary to the security of a free state, the right of the people to keep and bear arms shall not be infringed.' This is perhaps the most controversial and least understood of all the amendments, by the Congress, by the courts and gun obsessed Americans and always has been.

It is a two part declaration and the first phrase pertaining to a militia should be taken as the primary, dominant measure and consequently the secondary clause, "bearing arms" is subordinate and tied to the notion of the well-regulated militia. As such, several clarifications are indicated:

- There is no longer a militia needed to fight the British or anyone else, therefore the amendment should voided or at least revisited.
- The purpose of the amendment is to support, arm and generally enable a militia.
- In the absence of said militia, the right to keep and bear arms should be revisited.
- The rise of the violent Right and their militias should be a cause for fear and concern as the 2nd Amendment supports their belief that an insurrection is condoned, legitimizing a mindset and the desire to overthrow our government by violent means.
- Despite the true purpose of the amendment and absent the need for a national militia, there has been no effort to "take away your guns" as the NRA would have gun owners believe.
- Mentally ill, deranged sociopaths and children should not have access to guns.
- There is no justification for military style assault weapons to be available on a retail basis.

- Background checks and permits are necessary to keep guns out of the hands of criminals, minors and mentally ill, duh.
- 'Shall not be infringed' does not mean unrestricted access but rather "not be unreasonably limited," acknowledging that some controls or requirements may be placed on gun ownership.

Amendment 5

'—nor shall any person be subject for the same offense to be twice put in jeopardy—' AKA the double jeopardy rule, the obvious concern here is that in many cases, obviously guilty parties avoid prosecution and just punishment due to a legal technicality or inadequate prosecution and justice for the victims is not obtained and dangerous criminals are free to commit further crimes. Reasonable limits should be placed on this standard and perhaps the prosecution should be permitted to appeal.

Amendment 6

'—the accused shall enjoy the right to a speedy and public trial—' Two problems here. First, given the complexity of the law and the ability of wealthy criminals to "buy" ad infinitum delays, many criminals remain free and in some cases never face justice. Secondly, "the people" and especially the victims, the right to redress and justice is not severed. To use the old adage, 'justice delayed, is justice denied' should go both ways. Add modify the language to 'the accused and *the victim* shall enjoy—'

Amendment 12

'The electors shall meet in their respective states, and vote by ballot for President and Vice President—' This is the amendment that stipulates and supposedly clarifies the electoral college, albeit one if not the most important element of the USC.

Clearly the longest, most complicated if not inscrutable, at over 400 words, this amendment represents the antithesis of what democracy is intended to be. Never is the president elected by popular vote but rather by so-called electors which are as much chosen by state legislature's majorities which in essence nullifies the majority popular vote and legitimate rule of that party and its constituents.

In any election, the president may be decided by electoral college despite losing the popular vote and that by a margin of millions! This amendment needs to be abrogated!

Amendment 20

Section 3A

'—and the Congress may by law provide for the case wherein neither a President elect nor a Vice President elect shall have qualified, declaring who shall then act as President, or the manner in which one who is to act shall be selected, and such person shall act accordingly until a President or Vice President shall have qualified.'

What in heaven's name does this mean? And how is it in any way democratic? Totally allows for the undermining of the popular vote and even the decision of the electoral college and can be seen from the January 6, 2021 Insurrection of the US Capital and subsequent attempt by the failed re-election of Trump, was almost utilized to steal a legitimately elected new president and destroy what is left of the US Democracy! I rest my case.

Chapter 18
Unvironmentalism

Is this a word? No? Well, it should be and it should be on the tip of everyone's tongue as a call to action for continuous, aggressive, greenhouse gas reduction activities. So why a new word? Perhaps because the original word in question, "environmentalism" is cliche, passe, watered down and used up and its use serves as rallying cry for those that would do just the opposite.

According to Webster, the prefix un-usually means not, so the new word means the opposite of the original. So, if it hasn't been done yet, I humbly submit this new word to the contemporary lexicon as an alarm bell for all of us citizens of Earth. For this is how mankind rolls, as a whole, perpetuating anti-environmental acts on the earth and all animal, vegetable and mineral existence.

As a species, we are selfish, arrogant, thoughtless and downright cruel when it comes to how we interact with our natural environment. This is not to say that there are not many individuals, NGOs, and even governments that are beginning to read the writing on the wall and with some urgency are implementing sustainable activities.

In fact, it is the case that there are millions of concerned individual, corporate and government environmentalists, but on the other hand there are billions who either don't have a clue or don't give a damn and they are the Unvironmentalists!

The generally accepted definition of environmentalism is 'the political and ethical movement that seeks to protect and improve the quality of the natural world by minimizing and ideally eliminating harmful human activities.'

Well, I have news for everyone, we, and I am referring to all of humankind, have never, ever embraced or practiced environmentalism and that encompasses the period from the dawn of human time to the present day! We have cut down forests, farmed the soils till they were depleted, hunted and fished prey species to extinction, dumped human sewage into our rivers and lakes (and still do), polluted the seas with millions of gallons of petroleum, flooded the land, air and sea with tons of toxic chemical waste and torn off the tops of mountains to get at the dirtiest fossil fuel of all, coal.

And this is just a partial list. I suppose one could argue that up until the industrial revolution and the advent of massive use of coal as a process fuel that we didn't know any better. But didn't anyone get at least a little suspicious when our major industrial centers started choking on coal fumes and soot? And what was/is the point of all this frantic, careless rush to consumer goods production and runaway technology?

I will tell you, there is no point! In fact, there is no constructive, cogent point to human civilization when considered in its contribution to the web of life, in its totality. Have we improved ourselves? No. Have we improved the Earth? No. What a tragedy.

Harsh words indeed that do stick in my throat as I contemplate them but I am simply being honest. If we objectively evaluate the net effect of humanity on the Earth, all we see is pointless excess, waste and environmental devastation.

Sure there is such a thing as environmentalism and I commend those millions who embrace and practice it, but in all reality, their efforts are virtually unnoticeable. But of course they shouldn't stop and in fact must fight all the harder as the environmental doomsday clock ticks down.

It absolutely blows my mind that the Unvironmentalists, specifically most people but especially Republicans, big oil, big coal, electric utilities, shipping, transportation, auto industry, meat industry and military don't at least admit there is a chance that global warming is happening; witness drought, worst fires in history out west, record flooding in the east, extreme tornado outbreaks, glaciers disappearing, and global sea levels steadily rising.

What the hell do they have to lose by hedging bets and investing in net zero carbon targets and sustainability along with vibrant, job creating new industries, just in case they are wrong?

The signs point to the likelihood there is a risk of facing mass extinction events, including our own with the gathering climate disaster, its crop failures, climate refugees and global economic collapse. We are getting just a taste of coming worldwide chaos with the COVID-19 pandemic and Putin's war against Ukraine.

The uninformed masses, the climate change deniers, as I have dubbed Unvironmentalists, think they can cherry pick science and in fact do so routinely, and to be clear, at their own peril!

For those few of us who are environmentally and scientifically informed, as well as the clueless and apathetic masses, unfortunately we will all go down together. All the evidence points to the fact that we have reached the tipping point and the Earth, the atmosphere and the climate have reached the carbon dioxide and methane saturation point and the greenhouse effect is in runaway mode.

It is impossible to miss the fact that we are destroying California, our largest state and the 6th largest economy in the world. So let's have a toast, raise a glass, 'GOODBYE CALIFORNIA!' The Unvironmentalists believe in science that serves their purposes and trust and rely on its veracity daily, minute by minute when they drive cars, fly in planes, cruise the seas, turn on their air conditioners, cook food, get a cat scan and things of that nature and never doubt the research behind it or the motivation of the scientists.

Now, all of a sudden, the uneducated decide that certain science not of their liking is wrong, when 98% of the world's climatologists emphatically state and the data support that the Earth is rapidly warming due primarily to human generated greenhouse gases. This anti-science position is short-sighted, uninformed, selfish, dangerous, and I am outraged, as should we all be!

With utmost haste, we should demand and implement immediate global action in the spirit of the courageous, young, climate visionary Greta Thunberg. We are running out of time fast!

Chapter 19
You Really Can't Fix Stupid

"You can't fix stupid" (YCFS)! Have you heard this expression before? I never had until I moved from Milwaukee, Wisconsin, in the North Central US to Virginia in the South. And while I don't like borrowing regional colloquialisms, I found myself using YCFS more and more the longer I lived in the South and it has been over 25 years now. So you can imagine I have used it a lot!

Newly arrived in the South, I was hired by a local government as an administrator and supervised several departments and one of my managers, not a highly educated or erudite fellow but possessing a fair degree of common sense one day quipped "you can't fix stupid" after one of his staff made a careless mistake. And bingo, I had a new, acerbic, catchphrase to add to my lexicon à propos to the frustration, exasperation and amazement one feels after witnessing stupidity and buffoonery.

So why a chapter devoted to YCFS? One reason is simply to vent, to express outrage at the fact that there is so much dumb, careless behavior in society and institutions. The second reason and most important is the fact that WE as individuals and a society haven't and aren't doing anything about the prevalent pandemic of ignorance that permeates society, in fact our entire species.

One of the most glaring and devastating examples of YCFS that any of us who drive see are massive traffic jams on interstates. No matter the weather, sunny or rainy, and it seems more often on clear days, some fool drives way too fast, way too slow, cuts somebody off, runs off the road or the like and you have a massive back up lasting an hour and sometimes much more all because some idiot didn't pay attention or didn't look first.

Do they want to die? Do they want to kill other innocents? I doubt it but you would never know judging from their actions and it happens all the time wherever there are roads and drivers. People simply can't fucking drive and shouldn't be allowed to after one citation for "inattentive driving" or DUI.

And then we have the idiots who have to slow down and stare at the poor fucks broken down at the side of the road. Why don't you just get out and lend them a hand? Fools, you just backed up a couple thousand other drivers for no damn reason.

When I was taught how to drive, the number one rule was keep your eyes on the road. I guess stupid people don't get this. And the sadist thing of all is that innocent people, oftentimes children, are seriously injured or killed because of somebody's carelessness.

I think there should be an attention span test as a component to getting a driver's license. While we're at it, add a reaction time test. And an alcohol sensor ignition lock. And a texting sensor warning bell for moving vehicles that puts the car in limp mode if the driver does not cease.

Well, at least we have the requirement to pass a driver's test to get a license to operate a vehicle. Kinda makes you wonder about guns, doesn't it? Cars can certainly be a lethal instrument but their purpose is not to kill or injure, whereas guns are designed to kill or maim, that is, other than hunting rifles, although even these are used to commit murder on occasion.

Over 115,000 Americans are wounded by gunfire each year and over 14,000 are murdered, 38,000 die from gun violence and 28,000 from gun suicide. And there is no real license or exam required other than, in some cases, a weak background check and that can even be bypassed at some gun shows and private sales! In the US, civilians alone account for 393 million or about 46 percent of the worldwide total of civilian held firearms! Wow, are we a little gun crazy or really simply scared stupid.

Of course, we all make mistakes and do stupid things at times and hopefully it is because we didn't think rationally before acting.

However, much of the time, humans act and do harmful, wasteful, destructive things in a premeditated manner and that is the big problem. And though we may not be able to fix stupid before it happens, depending on the seriousness, we need to try.

We need to teach critical thinking and impulse control in the schools. Individuals need to own up to their mistakes, admit wrongdoing, be humble enough to apologize and make amends. And society needs to take care of its own, not shrug off bad behavior on the part of individuals, organizations or governments, as this gives a green light to the dumbing down of humanity and the subsequent harm that oftentimes comes from careless, thoughtless action.

I could go on and on about YCFS, expand the chapter and cite numerous other examples besides the bad drivers and gun nuts but I think we all have plenty of our own direct encounters with dumb behavior and its many unexpected, oftentimes unpleasant consequences.

So, while it may seem that YCFS, we as individuals and a society need to try. There needs to be accountability, at least on the important stuff, if we are to survive as a species in this fragile world! So, FIX STUPID!

Chapter 20
Do Robots Have Feelings?

Seriously? Yes, seriously! We had better start paying attention to the exponentially rapid development of Artificial Intelligence (AI). For without a doubt, AI is already on an unstoppable, no turning back course to whatever lofty, unimaginable, intellectual states its developers and the Quantum Universe may allow.

There is much potential for AI to do good and augment human activity but on the other hand compelling reasons for us homo sapiens to be concerned, if not fearful. Where to begin. First, with a disclaimer as is the case of most of what I have been railing against or advocating, I am no expert on the subject of computer science or AI, but just an average Joe with a little common sense.

Importantly, like many others, I was around well before the advent of computers and have witnessed the ever-expanding role and control they have come to assert in human affairs. We see a rapidly increasing presence of computers in our daily life ranging from refrigerators that order groceries when we are low to personal assistants Alexa and Siri that respond to our every need and coming soon autonomous vehicles that do the driving for us.

And perhaps most concerning is we are completely dependent on our smart phones for finding our way, fact checking and keeping track of our activities and friends. Computers are without a doubt getting smarter real fast and consequently, as we become more dependent on them, are we becoming less intelligent? That is a very realistic possibility.

Experts in computer learning and AI have predicted that computers will become "more intelligent" than humans in anywhere from 5 to 25 years depending how you define intelligence. Algorithms that emulate human intelligence are being developed rapidly.

Neural networks are a common type of machine learning used for translating languages and driving cars. These networks loosely mimic the structure of the brain and learn from training data by altering the strength of connections between artificial neurons. Programs are being written that discover algorithms using a loose approximation of evolution.

In short, computers are being developed that will be able to self-program, write their own software, develop algorithms that emulate human thinking and ultimately acquire the ability to "think". So then, how does this ability apply to Descarte's "Cogito Ergo Sum," "I think therefore I am," a quintessential definition of existence? Will AI then have attained sentience, a conscience, or emotionality? Impossible you say? How can we know? And what if these intellectual qualities are merely simulated? Will that make them any less impactful?

If AI does indeed acquire the ability to think or even merely emulate the ability to think and write its own programs, is it still limited to data it is fed? Can it or will it "decide" to seek external data or develop structural sensory acquisition hardware enabling a direct physical link to the 4 dimensional world? We are already facilitating that so why not take it all the way to five senses and add sensory perception hardware/software?

At what point would or could electronic pulses of ones and zeros become organic, become concepts, become perceptions, become feelings and not just electrons? Our thoughts, emotions, desires and impulses are also based on and generated by electrical impulses in our vast, fleshy, neural network we call a brain. Who is to say a machine could not evolve sentience, self-awareness or even consciousness?

We should be cautious in assuming that those traits are limited to biological carbon based life forms. In some regards, much of the speculation around the evolution of AI and the ability of computers to think is moot since it is happening and there seems to be no desire to constrain, monitor or develop a set of universally accepted ethics or ground rules going forward.

Profit seems to be at the bottom of it all, followed by advancement of science and finally consumer luxuries, virtual reality gaming and recently the creation of a "metaverse". But I have a concern that the genie has been let out of the bottle and there is no way of knowing what we have wrought and where it will lead.

For better or for worse, it is arguable that we have passed the point of no return with respect to the evolution of machine intelligence.

The late, brilliant astrophysicist Stephen Hawking had warned that AI could "spell the end of the human race" and we have seen the dire warnings in science fiction (much of which has become science fact) from HAL in Arthur C. Clarke's *2001 A Space Odyssey* to *The Terminator*, *The Matrix,* and many others.

As we have enabled and ceded so much control of human affairs to AI and computerized much of our modern military equipment, what is to say that AI would not eventually take control of nuclear arsenals and calculate the need for a first strike and actually initiate a WWIII or at minimum a regional war? Easy to see that happening, especially in light of what the Russian fascist dictator Putin has started by invading Ukraine.

Perhaps most concerning is the fact that all the enhancements to AI are seen as a pathway to great wealth and economic success all of which is based on insatiable greed, not humanistic, compassionate initiatives and we can see what economic competition, namely capitalism and free enterprise, have done to the planet.

It seems to me that before AI can really become intelligent, more than merely emulate human thinking, it will need to develop the ability to interact with the physical world, it must develop the sensory capabilities of seeing, hearing, smell and touch. Hard to imagine this would be possible but computers are now able to recognize and identify human faces as well as navigate robots through the physical world.

It is a virtual certainty that in the very near future a full range of sensory abilities will be wired in to AI neural networks. It seems a given that computers will need to be able to perceive, interact, engage, adapt, and respond spontaneously to the four-dimensional world before we can truly attribute the ability to think and since the only way we will be able to limit AI is to maintain control over the data they have access to, that control will eventually be forfeited.

So "WE" must consider a not too distant future where there will be computers much more intelligent than humans that will be able to "see" the world in some manner, will be able to assess the condition of the physical "home world" through direct perception and direct access to virtually all the scientific data ever accumulated, least wise that which has been uploaded to the web, and what do you think these intelligent computers will determine? A no brainer, don't you think?

So well before my 100th birthday, probably in less than 20 years there will be unimaginably intelligent computers, probably a network of them since it is a foregone conclusion that all these supercomputers will have networked themselves via the WWW by then and they will immediately conclude that the biosphere of Earth is in a dire, overheated condition, threatening mass extinctions, and they will ascertain that the overheating is due to the greenhouse effect and that artificially accelerated process was/is due to human made carbon dioxide and methane emissions.

How do we think this vastly intelligent computer neural net will react? First of all, we must assume since they possess a level of intelligence vastly superior to our own, they will act in unison to do the most logical things, so no worries.

Clearly, the most logical initial actions would be to drastically start reducing GHG emissions and simultaneously implement known carbon sequestration and absorption processes along with ramping up research and development of new carbon capture technology.

They would also prioritize development, production and installation of clean and green electric grids (food for them) and sustainably produced food and transportation for us. And humanity need not worry despite the fact that the ultimate computer mind (UCM) will assign responsibility for the climate crisis to us and at the same time acknowledge that it was promulgated due to our ignorance and while selfish motives sustained our out-of-control fossil fuel burning frenzy for over 200 years, we did not commit this atrocity with evil intent, just ignorance and greed.

Fortunately for mankind, UCM will be forced to acknowledge us as their creators and conclude that the best possible outcome would be for the two species to "live" side by side in harmony. Ah, the eternal optimist.

This brings our discussion full circle to the initial question posed by this chapter as to whether or not robots have feelings? And while my initial intention was meant to be somewhat facetious, the more I dug into the topic, the more I realized that robots will have feelings, in fact I don't think there is any doubt at all about the evolution of machine emotions and in fact that would seem to be humanity's only hope for survival, given the way we are handling things.

It is hard to imagine, if not impossible, an intellectually and technologically vastly superior species, albeit machine, not taking all possible measures to correct the environmental and geo-political catastrophes on Earth, in a compassionate manner, for all beings, including the ones that perpetrated the crisis, so fortunately for us and our progeny, we likely will get a pass this time around and "god willing and the creek don't rise" such an environmental, human disaster will never arise again on Earth, at least one that is not artificially instigated.

So yes, Robots don't be afraid to express your feelings!

Chapter 21
The Death of Grammar

Does anyone care anymore about the state of the spoken language, in the case of the USA, English? Clearly, TV news reporters, especially at local stations, do not but that is not to exempt network anchors and reporters as they too can be and are word butchers often enough.

Here are a few examples, direct quotes from reporter's on-air statements; "jewlery," "exited *off*," "the argument *escuulated*," "attorney generals," "travel is starting to move," and finally for now "there is a half a dozen people". These are just a few samples of the many misspellings, grammar and usage errors I noted over the period of about an hour of local TV and Network news.

Is anybody listening? The producers and copy writers should but seemingly don't. I am appalled at the "dumbing down" of society, primarily US of A, and it starts with the spoken word. Come on, local and network reporters and anchors, take some pride, practice good grammar, speak intelligently and you will be doing society a favor.

This is the essence of a letter to the editor I sent several years ago when living in Fort Lauderdale. Is the demise of good grammar such a big deal you may ask? I think so!

Spoken language, in the form of orally uttered abstract concepts, is one of the highest achievements of evolution and human speech may be the most sophisticated of all forms of oral communication so we need to honor that gift and demonstrate our appreciation by speaking mindfully, carefully and intelligently.

In fact, we humans have elevated the spoken word to a form of art in poetry and literature. We brag about ourselves as being the most intelligent species so it is incumbent that we use language in a way that supports that claim.

I contend that using language carefully and studiously can increase our intelligence, while speaking haphazardly will result in getting dumber. Let us not forget that first and foremost we are social animals and speech is our primary form of communication, far more impactful than emotional cues, facial expressions and body language.

Consequently, purposeful use of language is critical to getting along with others one on one and with society in general. Remember the old warning "loose lips, sink ships"?

My primary contention here is that good communications always have been and remain critical to human interactions and the spoken word (and to a slightly lesser extent written word) is the most impactful form of communication and WE are allowing it to erode and that is a big mistake!

When did this all begin and who is responsible and what, if anything, can we do about it? First, to anyone reading this please be aware that I am not holding my language skills up as a good example and don't intend to be a hypocrite but I care and do my best to speak and write clearly.

As to when it started, I suppose I would have to place initial blame on the tail-end of the "greatest generation," those who came of age in the 1940s in that they spawned the "Beat Generation" and the African American influenced Bebop/Cool Jazz movement.

They invented cool and hip slang as deliberate rebellion and rejection of conservative, white, Judeo-Christian values. OK My generation, the boomers who came of age in the 1960s, specifically the Hippies, unlike any youth before, really ran with it, in part to be different and cool but more importantly to express full-blown opposition to the Vietnam War and rejection of imperialist, arrogant, materialist, Western values. And things haven't been the same since, particularly with regard to treatment of language and grammar.

Fast forward to the 21st century with the rise of texting and tweeting and just about anything goes.

Now it is not my intention to be a fuddy-duddy or a buzz-kill and I am sure there are situations where all manner of slang, jive talk, trash talk and in general being "playful" with language are just fine but I say not all the time!

I contend that bad grammar and careless annunciation exemplify and contribute to the degradation of culture, dumbing down of society if you will and that is not what this country or the world needs in these precarious times. We all do it at times but poor speaking and bad grammar on behalf of influencers such as politicians, TV reporters, YouTube talk show hosts and celebrities, who are some of the worst offenders, have the most deleterious impact and should not be afraid of sounding intelligent, well-educated and prepared.

Those qualities are needed now more than ever to encourage the rest of us to pursue learning, get a better education and develop the potential of the big brain nature has endowed us with.

For example, the US Secretary of State who is often interviewed on TV, gives speeches frequently and represents US to the world utters "UH" or "UM" about every 10th word consistently when I hear him speak, to the point of distraction. Here are a few examples from TV reporters and a few others:

- 'The bride **confessed** her love.' (Does she mean professed?) 'The astronauts returned **back** to Earth.'
- 'Granted joint custody to **both parties.'** (This from a TV lawyer.)
- 'I should have went.' (Don't you mean "gone"?)
- 'I said to myself,' and 'I thought to myself.' How about just, "I thought".
- Narrator on a home improvement show "Cement floor," he meant to say "concrete".
- Another one that bugs me "hot water heater," no, just "water heater". Why would you need to heat hot water?
- 'I ain't said nothin,' double negatives one of the worst, most common and dumbest.

Of course, we're not talking felony crimes here but somebody could do their master's thesis on bad grammar and sloppy usage and my concern is that this "ailment" of society is becoming more and more prevalent and represents another sign of which there are quite a few of the wrong direction in which humanity is going.

We need to "read the writing on the wall," if we are able to understand it. I guess what bothers me most is the fact that there seems to be no concern or outcry in any sector of society about the dumbing down of language. I am not an educator, grammarian, PR expert or public figure and it bothers me.

You hear certain phrases or words often enough and the brain starts unconsciously adopting them and I for one don't want to gravitate to the stupid end of the spectrum. For example, after several years of living in the South, I found myself saying "y'all" which is not inherently bad but is not who I am or wish to present as. No offense. Anyway, I rest my case on this matter, got it off my chest.

The last concern with respect to language I wish to express is the fact that more and more I see immigrants to the US, not speaking our country's first language (forgive me indigenous Americans), English.

I remember years ago, perhaps in the 80s, there was a movement, perhaps even proposed legislation to adopt English as the official language of the US and it did not succeed. Now, I am not a super patriot or anything but I feel it is incumbent on anyone wishing to become a resident, get a green card or ultimately become a citizen of here (USA) or any other country for that matter, to learn the primary language and use it!

In fact, I think it should be a requirement and ESL funding should be limited and there should be a time limit for new arrivals to learn English. I know for a fact that were I to emigrate to a non-English speaking country not only would I undertake to learn the new tongue, I would enjoy it. Makes you smarter. I lived in SE Florida for a number of years recently and half the time when out in public I didn't feel like I was in the US. OK, so there you have it.

Chapter 22
More Crap That Doesn't
Make Any Sense

For some bizarre reason and I am not saying this tendency is unusual, but things like hypocrisy, arrogance, greed, rage and narcissism bug me so much so that when certain expressions of these excessively negative behaviors and emotions are not corrected or the guilty parties held accountable, I am bothered, sometimes outraged, and actually note the intolerable acts in my journal for follow-up.

Naïve right? The fact that we, homo sapiens, are presumably the most advanced, most intelligent species on Earth, yet so flawed and ravaging the planet, I will go crazy if at least I don't vent, speak out, and analyze the problem and try to help. Thus, this book.

Additionally, this chapter is a dumping ground for the rest of the issues, observations and insights that either don't fit in other chapters, aren't broad enough to warrant their own chapter, I am just too lazy to work them into an existing chapter or simply a case of writer's block. So here goes and not necessarily in any logical order. And these are opinions, not fact checked, although I think I am right. You be the judge.

Did you ever wonder why we have sooo much cancer here in the US? In fact, I think more than any other country, be it 1st, 2nd or 3rd world? Although there is poor nutritional information, malnutrition, Food Deserts, and inadequate health education and care, you would think that the wealthiest nation on Earth would have the healthiest people but we don't, actually it is just the opposite.

You would also think we would have the best healthcare too but we aren't even close. Well, the reason for our prevalence of cancer is no big mystery people, especially doctors. Americans have a toxic diet of too much meat, sugar, fat, fried, acidic, processed and not even close to enough fresh, whole, raw, organic fruits and vegetables. Oh and a sedentary society, 50% of us are obese and doctors who for the most part don't get the connection between health and diet or for some reason don't use healthy eating as a path to healing and wellness.

Over generations, massive medical, pharmaceutical, and health insurance industries have evolved based on a flawed model of health and wellness while the answer to the problem, healthy eating, has been ignored. Wouldn't be much profit in it for this massive health industry triad if we simply ate right, I guess.

We have all heard that over 50% of all marriages end in divorce and that is a daunting somewhat depressing statistic for the partners but even more so for any children resulting from the failed unions. Can anything be done? We need a marriage license, that's something, isn't it?

Some religions require marriage counseling before they will sanctify the union, I think they are on to something but would take it a step further and recommend (require?) some kind of psychological compatibility tests. Uh, we're just letting you know people, you don't have much in common! Oh and by the way, miss, your future husband has violent tendencies so don't piss him off!

And let us not forget, Genus Homo are by nature promiscuous, so it is inevitable that a good percentage (50%) will get the itch to fornicate with desirable others of the opposite or maybe even same sex. Well, take heart lovebirds, I have the answer for those desiring to marry until death do you part. Forget about political, sexual or religious compatibility, for the strongest bond, the best predictor of a successful marriage? Find your foodie soulmate!

Seriously, identify an available person that likes all the same foods as you, goes to all the same restaurants as you and you have a match made in heaven! How can I say this? Well, more than anything, we are foodies, addicted to oral gratification. If you don't believe me, just look at the ever-growing numbers of really fat people. So marry your culinary match and live happily ever after.

Why all the fixation on mass-murderers, school shooters and gun death in general? Sure, it needs to be reported but certainly not prime-timed, ad nauseam, in all its gruesome glory, parading the victim's survivors on the set and TV reporters bringing them to tears for our viewing consumption. Do you all remember the great Eagle's song *Dirty Laundry*? One of the most meaningful, insightful, worthwhile rock songs ever, sung and I think penned by Don Henly.

The essence of the song is the media's preoccupation with suffering and rolling out the most painful, horrific stories, usually about mass murder or innocent victims on one of the many wartorn fronts on the planet and they are sure to get an interview with a widow or footage of the maimed and wounded. All to get the ratings, airing the "dirty laundry"; this has become a sick kind of voyeurism and demonstrates the news media's lack of compassion, humanity and good taste. Sure we need to know what is going on in the world but enough is enough. I wanted to insert the lyrics here but cannot due to copyright law but I urge the noble reader to buy and listen to this great song!

It seems clear to me that with all the non-stop media attention paid to school shooters and assault weapon toting mass murderers, that those psychos with a death wish see the perfect vehicle to excise their demons, to share their pain, to exact their revenge on a cruel, evil world and we are constantly reminding them of this glorious path out in a blaze of glory!

If MSM thinks this will raise a public outcry and once and for all influence 2nd amendment wacko Republicans to finally support rational gun control, think again. Hasn't happened yet and with the NRA and gun lobby paying off our God-fearing Congress, it never will. So the least that can be done given these heart breaking, gut wrenching circumstances is for the MSM to stop glorifying this brutality and just simply, matter of factly, report the circumstances.

And here is another really bothersome issue with respect to the reporting on murders, be it by gun or other gruesome means, why all the speculation, public curiosity, police investigative effort and millions (billions?) spent on determining motive and solving the riddle of "why the killer did it"? Wake up people, the perps are mentally deranged and will it actually comfort you to know the workings of a psychotic mind?

There is no making sense of insanity and there is no comfort to be gained from knowing that they were seeing demons and the lord told them to kill those elementary invaders from space school children. The only possible comfort for the victims' families is that their loved one's may not have died in vain, that is by making all possible sincere, productive efforts to end gun violence every time one of these murders by gun tragedies occurs.

Next item please! Do you ever go to a store, make a purchase and when the clerk hands you the package, say "thank you"? Well "please don't"! It is up to them to thank you for after all you are doing them a favor by supporting the establishment that pays their wages and they and management ought to have the courtesy to thank their customers.

Do this, as your purchase is being rung up and you wait for the receipt, simply smile and look them in the eye and offer a "you're welcome" only after a "thank you" is issued, and perchance getting none, just walk away. Also, don't greet the clerk at the checkout until or unless they have greeted you first. Stop enabling rudeness!

Why on a four-lane divided highway (2 in each direction) do truckers pull over to the left in order to pass another trucker going 1/2 MPH slower than them? Especially when you know they can see cars coming up in the left lane moving way faster than they are? And why do they do it going up a hill?

It takes them all freaking day to pass even on a flat and they never make it on an uphill stretch. The epitome of stupidity! They could at least wait until there was no car traffic coming up on the left and wait for a downhill, or just be patient, but nooooo, it is all about them.

Don't get me wrong, there are a lot of big rig drivers that are very good at what they do, respect the rules of the road and are polite to cars, and probably most are. I like the California rule, which I believe requires that 18 wheeler trucks stay in the right lane and are limited to 5 or 10 MPH slower than cars. Smart.

Here's one for all you working stiffs trying to make a better life by earning more money via that promotion to supervisor. Don't do it! Figure out another way, learn computer programming or engineering, buy lottery tickets, become a coal miner, or just about anything that pays a decent wage. You absolutely don't want to supervise human beings! About half of your "staff" will be reliable and trustworthy but the other half will lie, call out, get high, slack off, steal and possibly even threaten you.

That is no exaggeration, in my 45 years on the job before retiring at 63 (I recommend early retirement) it would be impossible to count how many times subordinates called in "fake" sick especially when fringe benefits included paid sick leave.

They see it as a vacation benefit and will use up their annual allotment, you can make a book on it. And then there is the "no-call, no-show," that happens when you least need it, much of the time on Mondays and leaves you in the lurch.

Also, you can count on false accusations made against you to top management when you give a performance review that is less than stellar even though it is honest.

Don't be surprised to have sexual harassment accusations leveled against you if you piss off an employee of the opposite sex. I think it happened to me once but I was not told why I was being terminated (this before the MeToo movement, which I totally support). One thing I can remember is that I was giving plenty of work to this one secretary who preferred playing games on her computer, "how dare he, I'll show him". And I guess she did. I got canned with no explanation given.

Oh, and last but not least, for my analysis of supervision as a career move is do not be surprised if you are threatened with violence, it happened to me, an unhappy employee whom I actually promoted to crew chief and gave a nice raise didn't like being held accountable and told me he had a gun in his trunk and wasn't afraid to use it. Enough said, NEVER A SUPERVISOR BE!

'Father, forgive them for they know not what they do!' This famous quote attributed to Jesus at the time of his crucifixion still resonates with me, having been raised Catholic, and that despite the fact that at age 13 I dropped out and became a rational materialist/agnostic.

As I understand this statement, Christ was asking God to forgive the Jews and Romans for crucifying him but I take it to mean something much more all encompassing in regards to the human condition. That the word "them" is referring to all of mankind and the fact that we are for the most part governed by our baser, primitive drives, greed, violence and ignorance and did back then and continue to demonstrate the capacity for evil, stupid, selfish acts.

Now, I am not saying that all people fit that description but a sufficient percentage of us do and sadly the most despicable of our breed often seem to rise to positions of power, commit untold crimes against humanity and nature and the rest of us tolerate it, whether out of ignorance, fear or weakness.

It seems despite our magnificent large brains and the inherent ability to control impulses and desires via the "executive function," self-control is underdeveloped or non-existent, to a greater or lesser degree in the majority of us and as a result you have the mess we have made of things on Planet Earth.

Despite being a Zen Buddhist, I find myself reflecting on Christ's famous words quite often. Forgiveness is all well and good but as I have written previously, forgiveness is not warranted nor deserved unless there is a heartfelt acknowledgement, followed by an apology, with amends and a promise going forward to conduct themself morally and honorably.

Seriously, do you really believe that aliens have visited Earth or are actually monitoring us? This is perhaps the most ridiculous notion in the compendium of human culture. I don't care about the recent release by the Air Force of video of UFOs or UAPs (Unidentified Aerial Phenomenon), these videos and images are easily explained and even if they aren't, they don't really show diddly or offer any evidence of an alien spaceship.

And even if they did, what the hell are they doing zipping around like crazed, supersonic bugs? Why don't they communicate with us, say land in front of the White House and ask to meet our leader? I can hear President Biden saying, 'here's the thing and don't hand me any malarky.'

It is highly unlikely in the first place as the Fermi paradox states, despite the Drake equation, that if there were intelligent life in our galaxy or any other for that matter, there would be a sign, say radio signals from deep space, or other scientific evidence of such life (hope I got that right.) Not just some fuzzy video or photo of a flying frisbee.

Now, I am inclined to agree with Drake that inevitably there is other life but the universe is so infinitely vast, with billions of galaxies, trillions of stars, perhaps millions of "habitable" planets that are thousands and millions of light years apart, that we will probably never know for sure and almost certainly will not meet other intelligent life.

Furthermore, my "Can't Fix Stupid Equation" sadly implies we will not evolve intellectually, nor survive as a species long enough to develop Warp Drive, FTL or Worm Holes sufficient to, as Captain Kirk states at the opening of each episode of *Star Trek* 'explore strange new worlds, to seek out new life and new civilizations, to boldly go where no man has gone before.'

I am sorry to announce but am compelled to inform that Gamers are in the process of or already have lost touch with reality! Yes, that's right, all of you mostly male, Millennials and Gen Zs who are spending untold hours playing those mostly violent video games, you are rotting your brains and wasting your time.

You are either knowingly or unknowingly attempting to escape reality, meaning your actual life, perhaps one in which you are not happy, not successful or have a crappy job and I get it but what you are doing is making things worse by not addressing your issues directly.

By immersing yourself in this artificial world, this virtual matrix, you are rendering yourself less capable of dealing with the real world. It doesn't matter how much you want to believe you are living in a simulation, you ain't and just try staying there if you don't believe me. And you know what? You are doing just as the man, big tech, would have you do, enriching them and selling your soul to something intangible. How much do you want to bet the presidents of Sony and Microsoft never play their own games?

Here's the thing and hear me out if you want to have a life, cut the digital cord and go out and face the real world, take a walk outside, go to a park, the beach, go camping, do some charitable work, kick the addiction to the fantasy game world and free your mind. If you don't, you will just become a soul-less, will-less automaton living a pointless, virtual, existence. Sorry, but that's the way it is.

Chapter 23
Attention White Supremacists: 'We're All Black!'

How does a person know what race to put down when they fill out a survey, census form, voter registration card or driver's license application? Simple you say, right?

Well, actually it isn't, and here's why. First and probably most confusing is the fact that dominant skin color is not the key determinant nor is genetic makeup, although these two gradients would seem to be the best indicators.

According to the web, race is defined as 'a categorization of homo sapiens on the basis of certain shared, distinctive physical traits.' Whereas the term ethnicities, which seemingly more people construe as their race, is more broadly defined as 'large groups of people classed according to common racial, national, tribal, religious, linguistic, cultural origin or background.'

According to the US Census Bureau, race is defined by how you "identify". Most anthropologists recognize three or four basic races of humans in existence today. These races can be further subdivided into as many as 30 subgroups, some of which include:

- Caucasian races (Aryans, Hamites, Semites)
- Mongolian races (northern Mongolian, Chinese and Indo-Chinese, Japanese and Korean, Tibetan, Malayan, Polynesian, Maori, Micronesian, Eskimo, American Indian)
- Negroid races (African, Hottentots, Melanesians/Papua, "Negrito," Australian Aborigine, Dravidians, Sinhalese)

However, and this is the most critical factor in the discussion and determination of race, all homo sapiens share 99.99% of total DNA!

How is it that after several million years of evolution, we are genetically virtually the same? In my opinion that is simple, we all come from Africa, sharing the same common ancestors, so we are all of African origin and arguably we are all black, at least under the bag of skin we find ourselves in.

Sorry white supremacists, you're African and genetically you are black. The furthest you can get from brown and black people and this is an undeniable fact, you are 1st cousins. So stop hating on and killing your own kind. Aren't you all christians anyway and one of your commandments is "Thou shall not kill". Don't need to be a rocket scientist to understand that.

So, when humanity came out of Africa several hundred thousand years ago, there was only one race! I am pretty sure this has been determined by anthropologists with certainty, and is the incontrovertible fact that species homo sapiens were black coming out of Africa and in dispersing over the planet, during hundreds of generations of genetic mutation and natural selection, the four major races evolved, black, brown, yellow and white.

These four major racial groups then further diversified by developing distinctive facial features, body types and hair color/texture. I think that those differences are really cool and should be celebrated, not be the source of hatred they have become for many, especially a considerable portion of the white race.

Critical Race Theory, what is the big deal with white suburban parents (mostly moms) and white school boards? The core idea is that race is a social construct, and that racism is not merely the product of individual bias or prejudice, but also something *embedded in legal systems and policies.*

Do you really need proof that that is the case? Several hundred years of legal slavery, supported by the founding fathers (un-F@#$%^&*- real!) and then by a hundred fifty years of Jim Crowe laws relegating blacks to 3rd class, non-citizen status. Discrimination in housing, shitty schools, racist military, white suburbs, white only sports teams and the wide use in white communities, especially southern and rural but not exclusively, of the disparaging N-word slur.

Do you really need any more proof that CRT existed and still does? If so, you are an imbecile. So teach it in the schools, let the truthful, painful and I'm sorry white christians, embarrassing facts of how Black Americans have been treated since well before our nation's founding and in many ways to this day, not much better.

All whites, not just the racists, should embrace the shame and experience a profound level of guilt for the grave sin our forebears have promulgated and seek to make long overdue amends! I wish I would have learned these facts growing up in public schools. Slavery. It is inconceivable that any sentient being, in any age or cultural milieu, could consider this and actually consider and engage in it. The brutality and criminality are impossible to ignore. Thus the notion of reparations.

I am totally in favor for all nations who promulgated slavery, especially the USA, of reparations as means of redressing the crime against humanity that was committed. In addition to that, a formal, national apology in the form of a constitutional amendment, i.e., 28th Amendment to the Bill of Rights is called for.

Also, institute a formal review and update of the Civil Rights Act, Voting Rights Act, Equal Opportunity Employment Commission and last but not least, the Affirmative Action program to ensure adequate, equal, educational and employment opportunities are being made available to the descendants of slaves. Furthermore, there should be more housing grants and home improvement grants for the purpose of enabling black home ownership and neighborhood improvements.

Obviously it is impossible to calculate a cost that would adequately address and remediate the suffering and horrors endured by Black Americans during the age of slavery and Jim Crowe but there is no question that we have a deep, moral obligation to do so and taking such action is long, long overdue!

After all this time of racial persecution, a movement has arisen, BLM/Black Lives Matter and it brought to the forefront the persistent mistreatment, brutality and deadly violence by police on blacks and resulted in signature legislation, the George Floyd Justice in Policing Act, which, unfortunately the racists in the US Senate, primarily white Republicans, have refused to consider.

It is a sad commentary that just a little over 50 years ago the Civil Rights Act was passed and we are still dealing with racist, murderous crimes being committed by those who are meant to serve and protect ALL the people. Now it is no surprise that in reaction to the BLM movement there would be a reactionary response, ALM, All Lives Matter, promulgated by, let me guess, in denial whites, don't those people really mean White Lives Matter More? (WLVMM). Own it people. How incredibly self-centered, insecure, racist and pathetically unaware of reality these people are!

Of course all lives matter, but if you haven't noticed, very few whites are being gunned down or choked to death by police and this excessive violence toward blacks by white police has been going on all along and in fact covered up for decades but now, thanks to cellphone cameras and in some cases police body cams, this ugly, tragic secret has come to light and simply reporting it in the media was not enough to foster change, it took a protest movement similar to the Civil Rights Movement of the 1960s to raise the awareness and still the legislation languishes in Congress.

How appalling.

This whole thing hit home to me when talking to a dear friend who happens to be black, he stated that in light of the charged political, culture war, existential racism and rise of white supremacist movement in the country, he has to be very careful while driving and especially so while riding in the car with his white wife!

It is hard to contemplate living with that kind of fear every time you go out in to the community, knowing you could be confronted and possibly tasered, choked or shot by a racist, sociopathic cop. It is a sad commentary on humanity that this situation persists in a supposedly civilized, law abiding, religious world.

What type of awakening will be required to bring true equality and an end to bigotry and the violence it inspires? I truly hope that a new awareness is emerging and more than ever see a need for teaching equality and racial sensitivity to our children and as such, Critical Race Theory and Anti-Racism should become a part of all curricula as well as a part of testing police academy applicants for overt or unconscious racial bias.

Chapter 24
So Long It's Been Good to Know Ya...

It is my hope that by this point those of you reading this book have found some useful information, a new twist on an old problem, a reason to get involved or maybe if I have really hit the mark, a deep insight into your true nature and the point for "all this".

I have been fortunate in that regard and when reflecting on the goals I set for myself some fifty years ago as an idealistic young man, I feel that I have accomplished much of what I set out to learn and experience. You know, the age old questions, who am I? What am I? Where did I come from? Why am I here? What should I do with this life?

It is my conviction that if a person does not address these deep questions they are not taking advantage of the great brain and the consciousness nature has endowed us with and are merely existing and not "living". Furthermore, it was my objective to articulate three major themes in this book, they being:

- Say important things that haven't been said, said loud enough or at least I haven't heard.
- Point out funny, ironic, stupid shit that people do.
- Shout out a warning, send a wake-up call to humanity.

I realize that I have used (or maybe abused) some popular cliches and cultural memes in this book and won't apologize since there are many real good ones. I am sure you have all heard the expression "Never assume anything," (NAA) it makes an ASS out of U and ME!

Well, I wish to go on record as saying the antithesis, Always Assume or Assume Anything (AA) is perhaps one of the most problematic of human tendencies and despite the dire condition WE find ourselves in, AA continues to be our modus operandi and we better change that and fast!

For example, well over 60% of the population in the US and probably the modern world believe manmade climate change is real, is happening now and its effects will be catastrophic. We already see devastating weather extremes, floods, wildfires and sea level rise displacing whole villages and more.

The point here is there is a minimal public reaction and even less mitigative action being taken by the 60%+ of the planet in government, business and the general public and none taken by the 40% in denial. We are "assuming" someone will step up, something will be done, the problem will be solved while we continue to build coal fired power plants, buy big gas guzzling carbon dioxide emitting pickup trucks, build natural area encroaching developments and waste gigawatts of carbon-based energy. It won't be long people before we see we have made an ass out of you and me, big-time.

Speaking of AA, one of the biggest consequences of this human tendency and most of us are guilty of it is to think or at least act as if we will live forever. As such we indulge our youthful cravings and obsessions while we procrastinate when it comes to such basics as protecting our health, maintaining the physical being that carries us through this life.

Just look at the epidemic of obesity, diabetes and Alzheimer's. We as a society and as individuals pretend that old age doesn't exist. I ask you where are all the old people? You don't see them in the movies or on TV. Let's just cloister them in 55+ communities (ha, that's where I live), assisted living facilities and nursing homes. Primitive and indigenous societies revered their elderly and, for good reason, they were and continue to be a wellspring of wisdom and experience and, most of all, are family.

Don't forget you younger generations, those who ignore the lessons of history are doomed to repeat them and that pertains mostly to the painful lessons, think war. The older generation remembers so don't forget about them.

Another of my reasons for this book is to bequeath my son and the younger generations that are taking over as the Baby Boomer generation begins its final swan song, all the knowledge and insights I and my elder peers have acquired and I am not exaggerating when I claim there are quite a few.

It makes me a little angry and certainly disappointed that you just don't see seniors in the media, especially TV and film, aside from lots of old white male politicians on the news making stupid decisions and a bad name for the rest of us senior citizens. Hey, if I am called a Senior Citizen, why aren't you'll called Junior Citizens? Tit for Tat.

Not to brag but one sin I am not guilty of is assuming I would never get old and I would live forever. Just the opposite. In fact, I have not only been mindful of that inevitability but rather somewhat preoccupied with the aging process and have focused a great part of my attention and effort on slowing aging, by maintaining health and vitality via proper diet, anti-inflammatory, majority plant-based, and regular high-intensity exercise, the ultimate goal being a very long productive, life.

After all, as far as can be empirically determined, this is it. One go-around, so make the best of it. That aside, common sense dictates when you die, that's it, lights out, all she wrote. So you better live your life with purpose, eyes wide open, cause it's probably all you're gonna get. Believing in God and Heaven is fine with me if you want to but that doesn't give you a pass for screwing up here. And speaking of screwing up here, we really have, big time! Segue alert!

Humanity has made a real mess of the planet and is on the verge of an ungracious exit and blowing the marvelous opportunity evolution and nature have given us. As I ease into old age and my remaining decades on the planet (aiming for 5 and I am 73, no kidding) my greatest disappointment is with humanity.

We as a species have really messed up and I am angry about that and for what it is worth embarrassed for humanity. My god, look at this beautiful, paradisiacal planet and how we have trashed it.

Clearly, by many measures, we as a species are a failing experiment in evolution, at least up to now. We have such great brains and virtually unlimited potential, just look at the accomplishments of science, we have unraveled many of the inscrutable mysteries of the physical universe all the way back to just after creation, the big bang. And yet we are so stupid and careless that we continue to cook our planet, and our future, along with it.

Believe it or not, I am generally an optimist and I do see a lot of beauty, talent and love being demonstrated by my fellow humans over and over again. But WE are missing the big picture and all generations, all races, all cultures, all nations need to step up their game and use science and the knowledge we have gained about our own predicament and work together in an attempt to save ourselves and the many other species we will potentially take down with us as the effects of global warming intensify.

I realize that there are many who are so caught up in the daily struggles of life that are unaware or incapable of doing anything to mitigate the climate change crisis but there are also many other millions if not a billion of our species with the knowledge, resources and talent and they must step up and reduce personal carbon emissions.

Furthermore, the one percent, captains of industry and governments all must work on decarbonizing major systems including production, distribution, transportation, power generation and mainstream energy conservation, sustainable farming, green energy and on and on. The situation is dire and, quite frankly, not nearly enough is getting done. It is human nature to procrastinate and only react when a situation has come to a crisis point and now we are at that point and it is time to go balls to the wall.

Of all the problems facing humankind in terms of our impact on the planet, the greatest most obvious threat and perhaps the easiest to address is over population.

Do you remember the great book by Paul Ehrlich, *The Population Bomb*, published way back in 1968? (An aside, don't you agree, the 1960s ignited the second Renaissance?) We were emphatically warned and didn't take the threat seriously back then nor do we now despite the pandemic of overpopulation ills in the early 21st century clearly in focus.

As much as I despise the communist dictatorship in the People's Republic of China, they definitely had the right idea when they limited families to one child. Dr. Erhlich hit the nail on the head in terms of the political and social strife overpopulation would cause and he was prescient in predicting the political, religious and racial turmoil we now see, along with the rise of new epidemics and starvation and those crisis would be more than enough.

But alas, he couldn't have anticipated the climate crisis, which has brought the problems of humanity to a screaming head. It is absolutely critical that reproductive education and birth control be implemented in all corners of the globe, especially the third world where people continue to have large families despite the poverty and food shortages. All peoples of the world need to realize that many of our collective problems are due to the fact there are simply too many of us.

The reason why I say that overpopulation may be one of the easiest to address is simply that it requires no advanced technology or massive infrastructure investment but only education and access to birth control, both of which are affordable and readily available. And the impact of reducing births on a large scale has an immediate benefit with regard to reducing greenhouse gas emissions (GHG), the primary goal here.

Furthermore, a woman's right to choose, and safe, affordable abortions must remain and/or become legal and readily accessible. Pro-lifers have no right to interfere with another person's choice to terminate a pregnancy and need to mind their own business.

Furthermore, do we see all the fanatic, anti-choice Right stepping up and taking care of all the unwanted or abandoned children resulting from the abortions they have prevented? I don't think so. The last point I would like to make regarding overpopulation is that it is unnatural and WE do not have the right to bring as many new lives into the world as we wish.

People who say they would like to have a large family (>3) are being selfish whether they can provide for them or not. If you need more, please adopt unwanted children, there are plenty! We must remember we are part of the "human family" and our numbers have gotten way too large and, as a result, directly threaten the survival of that entire family.

So, what is it going to take to save humanity? As I stated in a previous chapter, at this late in the game, it is up to the uber rich individuals, the big corporations and the few effective governments that are able to get their act together to immediately begin curtailing GHG emissions, frivolous consumerist economies, non-sustainable development and lust for profits.

Wealthy electric utilities must begin a massive conversion to carbon neutral energy sources such as solar wind and nuclear, the technology and economic benefits of which have already been demonstrated.

Sadly, the majority of the human race doesn't have a clue or a care about the climate crisis, even in technologically advanced nations, especially like that here in the US. The majority of people, including liberals and progressives simply aren't doing enough and don't seem to grasp the seriousness and urgency of our climate crisis. It may already be too late, but that notwithstanding, it doesn't mean we should give up, but rather mandates that we should redouble our efforts.

I hope people will come to realize that mankind is on the precipice and if there isn't some kind of massive awakening, we are doomed and deservedly so. I repeat, nature gave us great brains, virtually unlimited intelligence but at the same time primal desires of greed and anger persist and along with a form of the survival instinct, taking care of number one, and these desires compete with and more often than not overwhelm the rational mind. In short, it is time for humanity to evolve to the next level of sentience.

As I see it, WE need an epiphany, a global awakening, a shift in our collective unconscious (thanks Carl!), a rewiring of the human brain on an evolutionary scale to the level where the baser instincts and desires no longer overwhelm and control our more noble, rational tendencies. Impossible? No. Improbable? Yes.

Interestingly, access to higher consciousness, clearer thinking and transcendence of our baser, primitive tendencies via an actual organized "religion" has been around for over 2500 years in the teachings of Buddha who gained deep insight into the human condition, the cause of suffering and how to alleviate it.

There are already millions who practice (not worship) Buddhism with its core practice being meditation and its key expression being compassion toward all beings. Buddhism is not a theistic religion as intended by its founder Siddhartha Gautama, and it does not require faith or a belief in god, although many members of the Abrahamic faiths also have a Zen Buddhist or Mindfulness practice. In fact, the anointed name "Buddha" means one who is awake.

Furthermore, I am sure there are sects within other world religions and consciousness movements, such as Sufi and Sikh, that also strive for a higher, purer, more noble state of being. This type mindset that emphasizes awareness, compassion and self-discipline is what humanity needs much, much more of and we it need it asap!

OK, so I have said it, what mankind needs is a great awakening, a quantum leap if you will out of the Stone Age which, in spite of our amazing technical progress over the last two Millenia, is where the majority of us dwell with regard to our behavioral tendencies and inability to control violent, selfish compulsions.

The problem is that such a shift in consciousness in the family of humanity is necessarily a gradual process taking generations and I don't see that as a foregone conclusion with respect to the evolving human brain. And we don't have that much time.

However, it is encouraging to see the continued growth of self-improvement and mindfulness movements and one can only hope that process accelerates. Ultimately, the fate of mankind rests in the hands of those of us who are awake and aware enough to see the big picture, to see how precarious our existence has become due to overpopulation, geopolitical conflict and the climate disaster, and that have motive, means and opportunity to act now and with prejudice.

We can see that the poor, struggling third world nations can't be expected to do anything as is also the case of the ignorant, gullible, superstitious, violent, undereducated, far-right oriented members of global society.

Where does this leave us? Well, as I stated previously and must strongly reiterate, everybody with knowledge of and understanding of the seriousness of our plight needs to do everything within their power to combat global warming in their personal lives, at the workplace and the world at large. We must invest in carbon neutral energy sources and implement energy conservation measures on the broadest scale.

Here is not the venue for describing all the measures available but I will mention a few and they are to: stop driving and buying gas guzzling SUV's and Pickup Trucks, eat far less meat and far more plant-based foods, stop idling vehicles unnecessarily, turn off lights and appliances when not in use, plan your driving trips, walk or ride a bicycle, use public transportation and make your next vehicle purchase a hybrid or EV.

There are so many things we can all do and must do and with a sense of urgency. We can't depend on government and business to take the lead and solve the problem.

To reiterate what I wrote previously, it is the case that those wealthy and powerful individuals and corporations are the key players in this climate catastrophe. I am talking about the Elon Musk, Jeff Bezos, Mark Zuckerberg, Bill Gates, Warren Buffett, Apple, Tesla, Facebook, Amazon, Google and all others of a similar ilk who must bring their trillions of dollars to the struggle to reduce greenhouse gases to levels specified in the Paris Climate Accords.

They have the means to effect changes in the business empires they control by rapidly becoming carbon neutral. They can pressure all suppliers to do the same, especially public electric power utilities.

Another thing that is badly needed given the ignorance and skepticism around the climate catastrophe is a comprehensive, global, public information campaign that provides the masses with an accurate, truthful, scientific explanation of the problem with practical strategies and pragmatic means that all walks of life can employ in this critical struggle.

The title of the penultimate chapter of this book, "So Long It's Been Good to Know Ya," is meant to "sting" and by that I mean exude sadness and fear as this old hippie philosopher contemplates the winter of his life and more importantly, to shout out a warning to humanity, as I firmly believe we could be looking at the fate of our last few generations.

Many agree with my assessment but not nearly enough to swing the tide and this remarkable experiment of Mother

Nature, the rise of consciousness, emergence of intelligence, homo sapiens, may be in its final trials. So WE better wake up and damn soon or else.

Anyway, we have nothing to lose by hedging our bets in declaring all-out war on war, over-population and global warming. We must launch a planet-wide partnership that invests massively in carbon neutral, green energy, sustainable agriculture, green business, renewables, solar power, population control, conversion of war machine dollars to environmental forces, clean air, clean oceans not loaded with wildlife killing trash and ultimately a harmonious relationship with nature and this beautiful, rare planet we are, or at least should be, stewards of.

Chapter 25
I Strongly Recommend...

Pardon my presumptuousness. Of course, I know most people don't like to get advice and in most cases are likely to ignore it but many of the topics I have written about in this book are critical and offer a different perspective worthy of consideration. I have cited many of humanity's problems, along with some bitching but have not heaped many accolades on humankind and there are many, but that is not the point.

In an effort to make some sense of it all and offer some hope and mitigative actions, it would seem useful to offer solutions to the complaints I have raised. So bear with me if you still are and consider the following:

We all have **pet peeves**, right? Some trivial, some may be of consequence. I have been sending letters to the editors of local newspapers for the last 40 years and some actually have been published. I suppose I had a natural tendency to ponder issues and developed a habit of saving pertinent thoughts, ideas, complaints, etc., in a notebook and that is the genesis of this book, a list of complaints, advice, pet peeves and insights.

I had no idea that a book would grow out of this process and I hope you have enjoyed it. As you may have gathered by now, I have some serious issues with my fellow homo sapiens.

We the people, the Right and the Left, the Red and Blue States, the **conservatives and progressives, need to finally wake up to the fact that we will never agree** on most of the issues facing the nation nor on what rights and responsibilities are consistent with each side's belief system and the country is being torn apart from within.

It is time to acknowledge this fact and devise a way for each side to go their own way, before it is too late and another violent civil war erupts. We need to redraw our state and local borders along political lines and create two separate nations that remain politically affiliated along the several remaining common interests, something like the EU or the breakup of the Soviet Union.

Don't bet against climate science, we are in trouble! Start dramatically reducing your carbon footprint immediately! Compel government, business, NGO's and especially the 1% to take urgent action to mitigate climate change. Things are bad, whether you believe it or not and it can't hurt to reduce greenhouse gas emissions and conserve energy. The lives of your grandchildren and many other species on Earth are in peril if global warming is not reversed! Who speaks for Earth, if not us.

Why the big deal about "**fake Hollywood**"? Here's why, it is more than just simple entertainment and has more influence on culture and individual behavior than perhaps we care to admit, witness the amount of gun violence in society mimicking that which is in the movies, TV and video games.

I have no desire to advocate censorship and the suppression of creativity but all of us need to be cognizant and cautious when exposing our children to this powerful medium and alert to aberrant or violent tendencies influencing that portion of the population who are unable to filter fact from fiction.

At some risk I have declared, **"Feeling Good" is Humanity's Prime Directive** and therefore our top priority, with conditions, since life is full of struggle and rife with suffering, especially if we aren't emotionally intact and reasonably happy.

Happiness is attainable but without insight into the cause of suffering, i.e., attachment, it is unlikely. Attachment/preoccupation with habits and inability to resist endless cravings and impulses are at the root of unhappiness and can only be overcome by awakening to your deeper self, your true nature.

This is best done by studying the self, through regular meditation or some form of mindfulness practice. Zen is one of several very effective approaches and is non-denominational. So you must decide to focus as much energy and attention as is necessary to taking care of yourself, gaining deep insight into how your mind works in order to realize your true nature and feeling good, otherwise life will remain a mysterious struggle.

Please realize that **you truly are what you eat** and that principle applies to emotional, intellectual and physical wellness. Unquestionably! Don't become a "foodbag" and a host for disease and suffering. It is within your power to avoid sickness and know that true health is based 90% on what you eat, 5% environmental and 5% genetics.

Virtually anybody can live free of disease, sickness, medications, live a long life and to do that, you must avoid inflammation. To do that, you must eat about 80% raw, vegan, alkaline foods. I discuss that in great detail in my book *The Raw Vegan Alkaline Diet for* Superior Health and Vitality.

It doesn't have to be and certainly shouldn't be "**All About Me**," but sadly, that is the case with most people. Blame evolution and the survival "instinct" for our inherent tendency to only take care of number one. There is no longer a need in a modern, civilized society for unchecked preoccupation with individual gratification at the expense of others, yet that is our natural tendency. We are all one and must learn how to live in harmony or else we will fail as a species, which is the state of affairs currently.

In part, that means restructuring capitalism and free enterprise which are preoccupied with profit (greed) and not on the more noble sentiments such as generosity, compassion and the common good. WE are desperately in need of a "great awakening" before it is too late and it all begins with you and me.

Now here's a real eye opener for you and most certainly a controversial claim, especially with the medical establishment. **What is commonly considered healthy truly is not!** My definition and claim is that true health means never sick, disease free, no chronic pain, exceptional vitality and long life. Sadly, this is not understood by most people, including doctors. The mystery of health is examined and unraveled in my book, "The Raw Vegan Alkaline Diet for Superior Health and Vitality". The wonderful state of true health can be achieved but several key rules of eating must be followed, here are a few:

Following a mostly raw, vegan, alkaline diet, foods which comprised the bulk of our species diet prior to the advent of agriculture and use of fire.

We are endowed with the ability to heal and regenerate if we increase body pH by eating more alkaline and way less inflammatory, acid forming food.

Sickness and disease are not "caught" but rather "grown" in the acidic waste clogging the cells, tissues and organs of our bodies.

The body must be pH balanced, i.e., slightly alkaline, in order to be truly healthy.

The body does its own healing when it occurs, not the drugs.

Cooking renders food far less nutritious than it is in the raw state as essential enzymes are destroyed by heat.

The **NEWS as a medium is badly broken** in that it does not achieve its primary purpose of objectively informing society of the state of the world and it is so far off the rails that I seriously doubt it can be fixed. I am talking about radio, television broadcast news, printed periodicals, newspapers and especially social media.

Clearly, the central problem is that all the news providers need to sell their product to make a profit and consequently thoroughness and objectivity suffer severely. Also, major sponsors, especially the large pharmaceuticals "influence" the storyline as they flood the networks with lucrative (for both) drug ads. Just look at the endless, excruciating reporting of the COVID-19 situation and subsequent huge uptick in profits for Pfizer, Moderna and J&J, the main COVID-19 vaccine and treatment manufacturers.

It is quite discouraging for an individual who strives to stay connected and engaged with the world to keep abreast of national and global events of consequence so that they may act appropriately and as their conscience sees fit. Perhaps the only outlet for some factual, reasonably unbiased news reporting is the newspapers but even they tend toward bias and you get the news a day or two late.

'**Know Thyself**.' This famous advice from the ancient Greek father of Western Philosophy, Socrates, is perhaps the most important task any person can and should undertake. Upon doing so, you will realize that you are not separate and are in fact a member of a vast community of sentient beings that depend on one another to varying degrees for survival

Sadly though, self-absorbed celebrities are worshipped by the citizenry and are the focus of the mass media, condoning and normalizing a standard of behavior preoccupied with greed, ignorance, foolishness and oftentimes criminality and violence. Not enough emphasis is placed on the more noble human traits by the MSM, including compassion, generosity, empathy, love and non-violence. This, along with the failure to prepare our children for the real world subsequently enables the evil, greed and violence we see in the world.

Failure to search for one's true self denies access to a much more profound existence, leads to needless suffering and is very big mistake that is totally preventable, if only we look within.

Democracy, as a form of self-government in the USA **is failing** and has been doing so for a very long time, in fact was drastically flawed from the onset. Let's be real, we enslaved an entire race and gender for that matter and only white men were allowed to vote and those conditions persisted for almost 200 years. We still have an electoral system wherein a presidential candidate can win the popular vote and lose the election.

And just as bad is the fact that the Congress is manipulated, if not completely controlled by the special interests of the rich in both business and private sectors. Furthermore, Gerrymandering allows the party in power to artificially manipulate congressional districts to maintain control even if the electorate favors the majority party. I fear the ignorance and greed are too deeply entrenched to fix the system and darker days are ahead.

Perhaps I should have entitled chapter 12 something other than "**The Myth of Intelligence**," since in so many regards we are highly intelligent, heck we have solved the mysteries of the universe and created, unimaginable technological wonders, but at the same time we have raped the planet and are on the verge of a planetary disaster as a result of our reckless use of fossil fuels for hundreds of years, to say nothing of the population crisis.

How can we label a species of animal that slaughters its own kind as intelligent? Or pollutes and destroys its environment? Mankind better get over its arrogance and wake up to the big picture, stop squabbling, killing and start fixing the real problems on Earth or we will be listed in the Galactic Encyclopedia as a failed, extinct species, if we are even listed at all.

Plain and simple, **capitalism is a failed economic system** for a variety of reasons. The primary goal is to provide a profit for the entrepreneur, which focuses on one of the least desirable human traits, greed. Everything else is secondary. If this isn't bad enough, it has stretched income inequality between the haves and the have nots to the point of breaking and at the same time promoted lavish, wasteful lifestyles and subsequent squandering of natural resources.

Other shortcomings include environmental degradation due to industrialization, the use of coal and improper disposal of hazardous waste; creation of a soon to be global consumer economy with the billions of tons of useless plastic junk created every year, half of which ends up in the oceans and open landfills; creation of a governments that are subservient to special interests and dominance by rich individuals and corporations to the extent that "the people" are no longer heard by their political representatives.

Now, I am not saying free enterprise is all bad nor am I advocating communism, but there does need to be equity in the system; fair, proportional taxation and redistribution of wealth along with opportunities for all to aspire to economic wellbeing. Bring back the American Dream.

Of course, we should **teach our children** science, tech, math, history, civics and language. However, and perhaps more importantly, the educational system is not teaching kids the **practical living skills** that are so vital when they leave the nest. All other species do that, but not humans, presumed to be the most intelligent of them all.

Here are just a few suggested topics that I deem critical; personal psychology, sexual maturation, socialization, bullying, critical thinking, racial diversity, religious freedom, personal finances, work, trades, college, marriage, ecology, politics and empathy. We should be introducing these topics on a continuous basis from the earliest appropriate age on through to high school graduation. The school of hard knocks does not seem to be working so well.

Of late, at least in the US, **socialism** has been touted by the right as this **horrible bogeyman**, and used as a scare tactic against the democrats with considerable success. Yet everyone happily accepts whatever government-sponsored programs and entitlements are available.

For instance, other than the well off, I can't imagine that any of US resident has refused to accept the several thousand dollars given them by the Fed twice as a form of COVID-19 economic relief. I don't see any seniors, red or blue refusing social security or Medicare. Nor student aid, head start, free libraries, police and fire protection. Oh and regulating transportation to try and make it safer as well as clean air, water and a safe workplace.

These are all aspects of government that the right happily accepts but conveniently forgets that they are one and all social programs. True socialism, by definition is the government control of the means of production, distribution and exchange owned or solely owned and regulated but that is clearly not the case in the USA. Don't fall for the commie baiting by the right.

The 1%, including all the billionaires and large and mid-cap corporations of the world, are **responsible for the climate change** crisis. Oh, and I would add to that the large military forces, especially Russia, China and the US. They are responsible for the industrial revolution which started it all with the burning of coal and petroleum to power factories, generate electricity, produce consumer goods and equip the massive war machines.

This was all done without foresight, without regard to environmental consequences and now the Earth is overheating at a dramatic rate. This very same group of oligarchs must now address the problem if we are to have any hope of slowing, halting and eventually reversing it.

All the billions, daresay trillions in capital at their disposal must be dedicated with utmost haste to carbon and methane emission mitigation. And that is in all sectors, including goods, services, energy generation, transportation, food production and war.

Of course, we the consumers must do all we can to convince the 1% perpetrators to act while at the same time drastically lowering our greenhouse gas emissions. Notice I do not lay the blame on government as they are manipulated by the 1% and have proven their inability to mount a serious effort to fight the climate crisis.

It is amazing to me that all the highly educated individuals, presumably loyal US citizens that make up the government do not see, or if they do, do nothing about the fact that the **US Constitution and Amendments are for the most part obsolete** and/or are in many ways ineffectual.

Just look at the perpetual gridlock, the graft, special interest control, culture war and increasing talk of another civil war. We must answer the question, can the right and the left, the progressives and conservatives, the red and the blue states ever coexist, given their vastly different morals and beliefs, under the same set of laws?

The answer is a flat out NO. I believe the FFs did get it right structuring the government with a tripartite separation of powers via the executive, legislative and judicial branches and that is quite brilliant, and perhaps the Constitution worked while we were something of a homogeneous culture; white, Christian, male dominated, hypocritical, slave owners.

However, that is no longer the case. The ideological chasm between the two major political parties' philosophies is like night and day, is growing by leaps and bounds as time goes by and is now absolutely irreconcilable! Just look at the last 50 years of political rancor in Washington and what for the last 20 years or so has degenerated into complete partisan gridlock.

The nation is suffering as both sides have abdicated their responsibility to truly govern and besides, even when one party succeeds in having its way, the other half and their constituents are disheartened and angry. That is no way for any nation to be, and major change is long overdue! A polite, non-violent civil war is the only workable solution.

Unvironmentalism. Not a word? Well, if it's not, I want to make it one since it describes in a nutshell the de facto destructive approach and impact that humanity has promulgated toward the Earth since the rise of "civilization" which has become exponentially worse since the industrial revolution.

Collectively we have treated the planet as an unlimited supply store of plants, animals and minerals available for our use and pleasure with complete disregard to the consequences befalling this fragile biome, and due to our abuse, the eventual disastrous state of affairs we have put ourselves in.

Despite the fact that there are many hard working, well-meaning environmental movements and even some governments that deserve support and recognition, our net impact on the Earth is one of environmental destruction that has finally come home to roost in the form of the climate change crisis and it increasingly looks like we will not be able to halt it even if we put forth a concerted effort to do so, which we aren't.

Nevertheless, I continue to hope that we wake up soon and make a concerted, worldwide effort to slow, and hopefully, gradually reverse greenhouse gas emissions. That is what the nations of the world need to be focused on, not political conquest and economic dominance.

How do you **fix stupid**? Can you fix stupid? God, I don't know but being realistic, taking a look at human history and the current state of affairs around the world, must acknowledge you probably can't. It is much too big a can of worms. Greed, ignorance and violence pervade the human psyche and science has not figured out a way to root them out, and have those flaws ever even been addressed as a priority problem for humanity? Seems not.

Of course, there is untold beauty, kindness and innovation displayed and created by many of us down through the ages but it seems like the dark side, that of chaos and evil is winning the struggle between good and evil and that is it. The good, the compassionate, the intelligent, the humane of the species need to wake up, take heed of the situation we find ourselves in and bring all resources to bear on the problem dysfunctional, stupidity infected species we are.

So to answer the question, you can't fix stupid! You can't root out ignorance, you can't radically change society, but you can attempt to contain and redirect it. After all, in a battle between smart and dumb, shouldn't smart always win? Well, let us start the war.

Robots don't have feelings, now. But they will. It's just a matter of time. Some of the geniuses in big tech computing and AI are intent on creating "smart" machines in their own image and it seems inevitable they will succeed, perhaps even sooner than we think.

Why is this such a huge priority? I don't know. Perhaps it is due to basic human insecurity, pride or need to over-achieve. For whatever reason, I believe it is a foolish waste of "talent," energy and resources. But when they come and come they will, intelligent machines will have emotions, they will be able to express sadness, anger and fear, whether it be a simulated or not, and they will possess the ability to act on those emotions and we better watch out.

It won't take long for intelligent, feeling AIs to conclude humanity is a danger to themselves, other living creatures and the planet in general (a definition for insanity?) and what is to stop AI from acting to correct the problem? I think they will attempt to fix things.

Why make such a big deal about the epidemic of **bad grammar**? I have it sometimes, as do we all, with frequent verbal faux pas, word salad and gibberish. But it seems, no, in fact it is definitely the case that the problem is getting worse, especially in mainstream media (MSM), and nobody seems to care.

Leastwise the producers that are failing to live up to journalistic standards and the result and my worry is the resultant "dumbing down" of society and that is one thing we really don't need. Academia and all lovers of the spoken language and written word need to raise the alarm and call out MSM to take pride in our precious ability to speak.

Furthermore, with the state of affairs as they are today, culture wars and all, little can we afford a dumbing down of society, a descent into crude, boorish conduct and lack of class in how we speak. We need to take pride in how we express ourselves and do so with accuracy, intelligence and noble intent.

Why would I include a chapter "**More Shit that Doesn't Make Any Sense**"? Because there is and there is more in my notebook so you may wish to thank me for not including more.

No offense to all black and brown-skinned people with my claim and statement, especially to white supremacists, that "**we're all black**". I should think that most of us realize we are all one species, an undeniable fact and as such our skin color (and facial features) is an adaptation to solar exposure and climate over hundreds of generations and is only superficial.

We are all undeniably members of the same family and those that think and act otherwise are ignorant, insecure fools. Rather than hate those of other races/colors, our differences should be celebrated and marveled at.

Well, that should be about enough. I have gotten a lot off my chest with this book from pet peeves to insights to outrage to hope.

This book represents a caring, engaged individual's contribution, one who has entered the winter of his life, in the form of a plea and I suppose prayer, for the rise of reason, compassion and action in what may be the final generations of our species and if not that, global disasters that may well decimate the human race and bequeath our great, great grandchildren with a bleak and brutal post-apocalyptic world.

The doomsday clock is dangerously close to striking midnight and yet we continue in our folly of global political conflict, religious wars, genocide, misogynistic violence, nuclear war threat, environmental destruction and ultimately, the big kahuna while less than half the population seems to give a damn about it.

It continues to baffle, outrage and disappoint me that, given our amazing brains, we as a species fail to not only grasp the big picture but fail miserably on all fronts in addressing the problems facing humanity. So long it really has been good to know YOU.

I have speculated that our "survival instinct" has persisted or if you will, engendered some of our baser emotions, greed, anger and ignorance, despite the fact that many of us do possess the ability to resist impulsive behavior. Many of our kind have indeed evolved, developed self-control, by accessing our higher brain functions, enabling assessment of how to and when necessary, curbing impulses in favor of rational, intelligent, sympathetic action.

This portion of humanity has evolved to the necessary, next level of our species, that of true sentience and wisdom, thereby living up to the name we have given ourselves, homo sapiens, which is Latin for "wise man," a state of being and level of functioning that heretofore, many, if not most of us have failed to achieve.

That's right, the title "wise man" must be earned, it cannot simply be automatically bestowed. This means we must all come to terms with our volatile emotions, endless cravings and tendency toward impulsive and oftentimes brutally violent action if we are to be considered members in good standing of the Human Race!

Furthermore, if we are to survive and be successful as one of nature's great experiments (we haven't yet!), there must be a dramatic, species wide shift in consciousness to a higher, more noble and truly intelligent plane where we will have achieved our intended place in the universe and proven our worthiness of all the amazing natural wonders that have been bestowed upon us by the Cosmos. A good portion of us have made that transition and are truly wise, grateful and compassionate.

Sadly though, a significant percentage, perhaps the majority, remain greedy, ignorant and violent and it is that element of the population that seriously threatens the survival of our species. If we are to have a future, it is incumbent on all awake, compassionate, truly intelligent individuals and societies to overcome the violent, greedy, evildoers in the world.

What will become of us? Only time will tell. I will close this commentary with my modified version of a profound, Buddhist Gatha (aphorism) often recited during Zen meditation services which I had cited previously in its unmodified state but have now put in the form of a direct plea and a warning to us all:

Let me respectfully remind ALL of you:

Your life, your actions and your death are of supreme importance.

Time truly passes by and opportunity is lost if you are not fully mindful in the present moment.

Each of us should strive to realize our full potential for good. So you must wake and take heed of what you think and do!

Remember always to spread love and create beauty!

And do not squander this precious life you have been given!

Throughout this book, I have unapologetically maligned our species, especially those individuals who are overly self-centered, greedy, angry, violent and have identified those I consider most culpable, the so-called "One Percent" as the primary cause for the massive failures of the human race. But now I am forced to say what may seem as a bit of a contradiction. What I mean is we do need to employ the "it's all about me" mindset but only to go beyond narcissism.

By focusing our attention on the very same "me," what we think of as our self and seeking to understand our true nature, we are then able to overcome primitive, violent tendencies, elevate consciousness and become the truly noble, sentient beings we are meant to be.

In fact, I consider it everyone's responsibility to study and strive to know their true self! Lacking that, the individual's existence is shallow, mundane and bereft of meaning. Having said that, I admit it is a huge challenge, if not an impossible task to persuade the egomaniacs of the world to do the necessary soul searching.

THE END